THE UNCERTAIN LEGACY:
VOLUME II

THE UNCERTAINTY OF ECONOMICS

TERRY FAILING

Volume one of this series discussed the uncertainty surrounding our various conceptions of God. Four siblings argue about which of their very different opinions is the correct one. Their father moderates the discussion with the intention of demonstrating that no one can, nor should be absolutely certain about the truth or adequacy of their beliefs or lack of beliefs in the matter. Unfortunately, two of the siblings stubbornly refuse to entertain any other possible interpretations of God than their own: a fundamentalist Christian minister, and an Atheist scientist. Another is willing to consider other understandings, but is vague and confused about any beliefs beyond the common new age cliché that God is love. The fourth sibling doesn't care what God might really be since the here and now of his current life trumps all other concerns. The first volume concluded with no solid answer regarding the nature of God, but it did establish the positive value in maintaining uncertainty, and avoiding dogmatism while still actively seeking answers to important and difficult questions. This volume addresses the same principle as they apply to economic systems and solutions. The shift from religious questions to economic ones is not as large as it first seems, since economic orthodoxies have become just as contentious as religious ones were in the past with wars now being fought over economic beliefs, economic heretics being attacked and castigated by their opponents, and many true believers taking their own opinions much too seriously.

These volumes take the format of a drama rather than that of an essay so that extreme views that the author would not normally take himself can be presented, and judged in an entertaining and dynamic manner. Also, writing a non-fiction essay which delineates which economic ideas and attitudes are good and bad would undermine the general purpose of these volumes: valuing uncertainty above dogmatism. The reader is left up to his or her own devices to determine where economic truths might reside.

Mission Impossible?

The nation's economic prospects seemed dark and uncertain. The smells of economic panic sometimes wafted out from obscure quarters and anyone with an opinion about the causes of this economic disaster were loudly broadcasting their theories about how to avoid it.

An old man sits in a library where books crowd dusty shelves that rise from the floor to the ceiling. While we can't quite read the emotions he is experiencing, he seems peacefully engrossed in the leather-bound book on his knees. He doesn't look up when a tall, well-built man enters the room. The young man fidgets for a moment before clearing his throat to get the old man's attention. The old man looks up and appears surprised at the interruption. His surprise turns to shock when he looks more closely at the man's face and perceives a mixture of fear and embarrassment. He has never seen his son exhibit such a combination of emotions before.

AL. Hi Pops. Uh, How've you've been? I was thinking. Maybe you could help me.

FATHER. Help you? I'm surprised. You need my advice? I think the last time you asked for my help you were about twelve years old. You haven't stopped by for even an idle chat much less ask for my help since you stormed out of here when I decided you weren't ready to receive my legacy.

AL. Well, I've done fine up to now without your paltry legacy. I've made enough to take care of myself without having to accept the doubt and uncertainty, which you seem to prize so much, and which you attached as a condition of your handout. But now I think I'm about to be voted out of office, and I can't think of anyway to prevent it. I've tried everything, every political trick in my playbook. Nothing works, so what the hell. I have nothing to lose by talking to you, and maybe you can think something up, or see something I can't see that will save me, or failing that, provide some of that legacy you promised so I can get by.

FATHER.(*Smiling*) Well, you do sound more uncertain than you've ever been before. Maybe.... While I never expected that you would ask for my help, I can understand why you are here. I've been reading about your problems in the newspapers. You and your fellow legislators have been struggling to set our nation's economy back on its feet, sometimes spending more time undermining and criticizing one other than fixing actual economic problems, which many of you seem intent on papering over rather than addressing directly anyway. (He looks at Al over the top of his glasses).

AL. (*Looking a little uncomfortable*) What economic problems?

FATHER. (*In a frustrated tone*) Well, how about the millions of discouraged workers who don't even look for work anymore, and as a result, don't show up in your official unemployment rate? Or how about the thousands of our manufacturers that have closed their doors and have either gone out of business or moved out of the country while you and your cronies crow about the few high technology businesses that have taken their place? How about the many homeowners who still hold mortgages that cost more than what their homes are worth on the open market? Yes, you and your comrades have created a tidy mess. I can understand why the public might not be too happy with you You've always bragged how much

2

you love to be faced with challenges. You must find the current economic climate very invigorating.

AL. (*Purses his lips and then smiles weakly*) Heh, it would be invigorating if I could think up a solution to these problems that the public would buy, but nothing I or any of my fellow legislators have tried has brought the kind of permanent fixes that satisfies the voter. I have proposed several solutions, but can't implement any of them because my opponents claim they will cause even greater problems than the ones I want to fix. My economic advisors tell me that my opponent's solutions are just as bad, and of course, I don't want to give my rivals any unnecessary credit even if their ideas are sound. The problems you mentioned only scratch the surface of the situation we face in Congress, and the solutions we propose seem to alienate one group or another the moment we propose them.

FATHER. It seems that you and your colleagues have been trying to calm a boiling pot of economic problems by stirring it in different directions. Of course the pot continues to spill over; perhaps because one person's efforts clashes with another's.

AL. That might be part of the problem, but to refrain from stirring won't keep the pot from boiling over either. I need a way to permanently fix the economy once and for all.

FATHER. Society is always faced with problems and challenges in one way or another in ways that no one can completely fix. You're searching for a remedy for an ailing economy that resists repair. I don't know for certain what that remedy could be. I'm sure someone else will appear who thinks they know the economic medicine that should be applied to make everyone economically healthy and happy, but you may find that after you have implemented their economic wonder drug and answered whatever questions you thought were holding back human happiness, you have only changed the appearance of the malady, and the logical elements of the question. You have to accept that you are engaged in a never-ending task.

AL. All I know is that I'm in trouble and I need some of that advice you were always trying to force-feed me. I'm now willing to listen to any insights you might provide if it can successfully get me through the next election.

FATHER. It sounds like the real problem you want me to solve is really your political problem, not the country's economic one.

AL. (*Smiling broadly*) If I'm not elected, I won't be able to do anything except watch from the sidelines. I can't live that way. I have to be always in motion. I need to be a player. That's what I am. You know that as well as I. I need an opportunity to beat the forces that are pulling the economy apart. I can't do that if I'm not allowed to play in the game. I need advice that will fix both my political problems and the country's economic ones.

FATHER. (*Somewhat sarcastically*) Knowing you, I'm sure you've already tried every political trick in the book to escape accepting responsibility for any attempt you have previously made to improve the economy that the public now views as unsuccessful. You might have done better if you admitted before now that you were not certain how to fix everything for everyone. I suspect that your own arrogant certainty that you could fool the public into believing that you had everything under control, and still escape from every mistake you made has brought you to this dead end. I know you wouldn't have come to me unless you had exhausted every possible political option. Now you want my advice about how to accomplish what you must admit is impossible. That's a pretty tall order.

AL. Er, something like that. I know how to deal with all the politics involved; I'm hoping you know something about economics that will help me out.

FATHER. I only know about uncertainty, and economics contains much of that. I can teach you ways to live with the inherent uncertainties of economics. Would that please you?

AL. That's not going to help me much. There is already too much of that going around. No matter what economic fix I propose, someone, sometimes from within my own party, steps forward to point out why it won't work, and frankly, their arguments sound just as believable as mine do. No matter what I try to do, I'm told that I am only making the situation worse.

FATHER. That's because, someone's economic interests, somewhere, somehow, will end up being hurt by any possible solution and their paid representatives in Congress will always step forward to defend their sponsors; as a career politician that should be no surprise to you.

AL. It isn't, but this situation is worse than usual If only one particular group of individuals were objecting to what I've tried to do, I could probably handle it. This time everyone seems to be unhappy no matter what I propose. Those who must give up something object, of course, but those who might gain feel that I haven't done enough.

FATHER. (*Nods and appears deep in thought*). You don't like being put into a no win situation do you? You don't know how to handle the uncertainty that such a situation presents.

AL. Of course not! I'm a natural winner, and I feel like I should know how to make things right, but I don't. Nobody does.

FATHER. Maybe you already know what you must do, but can't quite say just what that is.

AL. What the hell does that mean?

FATHER. Sometimes life's most obvious lessons are also the most difficult to locate, understand, and use. Sometimes they lie before us in plain
sight yet remain unseen. They have become part of the wallpaper of our
existence, or the background noise of every conversation. We have sifted
them out of our consciousness to search for truths that we think are more
useful and important because they appear new to us.

AL. I can see my problems quite clearly thank you. Thousands of my
constituents are still out of work. They need money to support themselves
and their families. So we extended their unemployment benefits and made
other public assistance more easily available. They take these benefits
but remain unhappy because they're still unemployed. These benefits
cost money, of course, and the only people with money are employers,
investors, and people with jobs. So we increase unemployment insurance
premiums on the employers and try to raise taxes from those who have
money to pay for the benefits, which makes both groups extremely unhappy. The employers threaten to move their businesses out of the country, (which they want to do anyway in order to lower labor costs), and
those people with enough taxable income that requires paying taxes fight
every effort we make to implement any tax increase. They don't want to
be penalized so that some other family will benefit, no matter how small
that penalty might be to them. Furthermore, some of these people have
convinced themselves that their objections to the assistance we have been
providing to the poor are not based on their own self-interest, and that
unemployment benefits and public assistance are moral evils that corrupt
the recipient's work ethic and public morals. When we try to fund these
benefits by borrowing the money to pay for them rather than raise taxes,
we are criticized by many in the financial community that the debt we are
incurring will come back to haunt us when it is time to pay it back. They
say we will spread the current economic and social pain we are avoiding
now well into the future. They say that the borrowing we are doing now
will raise interest rates for any future debt, and that these higher rates will
eventually choke off future business investment, force a tax increase to

pay off the debt we have already incurred, and possibly force a draconian reduction in future benefits to the needy because after the debt payments there will be no money left to help them. These critics predict a future economic apocalypse where everyone, rich and poor, will suffer. I can't successfully campaign in the face of such fear or against the prevailing attitude of "to hell with everyone else, but don't penalize me. Make someone else suffer and pay". This attitude seems to underlie most of the economic problems I need to solve.

FATHER. Then why are you trying to fix the economic problems? Why aren't you trying to solve your constituent's attitudinal problems instead?

AL. I want to be re-elected. Voters don't want to hear that they are part of the problem.

FATHER. In other words, you're as interested in helping yourself as everyone else is. Consider that you too might possess the same selfish attitude that has soured all your previous attempts to solve our economic problems.

AL. (*Thinks a moment, then weakly smiles*). Yes, I'm as guilty as everyone else, except I'm willing to help other people in order to help myself. I just don't know which people I should start helping first, or how to do it, and more importantly, how to keep the people I'm not helping happy in the meantime.

FATHER. Well, your level of altruism is under whelming at best, but at least you're really trying to understand and fix the economy. Since you can look at least a little beyond your own needs you might be able to craft some sort of conditional or temporary economic solution that most people will accept, unlike someone who could only see their own personal interests and problems. The fact that you admit you don't know how to proceed puts you in a more honest and productive position than others who claim to know exactly the one way to address a troubling and uncertain situation. You can benefit from your uncertainty because it will focus your attention toward solutions you might not ordinarily see. I'd advise you not to seek these solutions alone, however. Economic problems encompass an area well beyond any one person's or even one group's understanding. You need the assistance of other people.

AL. Well, I admit that I don't know what to do, Pops. In fact, I'm completely stumped. People claim to be unhappy no matter what policy I choose, and I don't see how I'm going to survive the next election since no one has any faith in me. My colleagues and I have allowed ourselves to be pushed from one side of the economic spectrum to the other and back again. Should we spend and tax more to save the economy or reduce spending and taxes instead? Should we regulate more to prevent one group from taking advantage of another, or should we deregulate to encourage free markets? We kept changing our minds. That's why we've alienated everyone. The people want certainty. They want a sense of immutability from our solutions, and the emotional glow of a feeling of being at rest. They want to feel secure that we know what we're doing. We don't, and now they know it. They feel we misled them.

FATHER. And so you did. You led them to believe that such certainty was possible and that you had constructed the final, perfect solution that couldn't possibly fail, when, in fact the nation's economy has grown too big and complex to be properly understood much less permanently fixed. Expressing any certainty about your economic remedies will eventually lead to the public's disillusionment when the economy has a relapse. You were trying to accomplish the impossible and crowing about your planned future success. History presents us with a long accumulation of ambiguities and inconsistencies of one disappointment following another mixed in with each success. While history never repeats itself exactly, you might have absorbed some useful wisdom if you had studied it more closely. I believe you would have found yourself in a lot less trouble with the electorate if you had persuaded them to acknowledge the uncertainty of their situation. To do so might have vaccinated them against future disappointment.

AL. That would never work. People expect the government to provide stability, not uncertainty.

FATHER. Stability and certainty are not the same. You can establish economic stability without proposing permanent economic solutions.

AL. It's a lot easier to convince people of the effectiveness of a solution if you present it as guaranteed to work.

FATHER. You're always trying to take the easy way out of any dilemma. Taking short cuts to garner your constituents' support can ultimately lead to their permanent lack of trust about anything you try to do. If you demonstrate up front that you expect the path to economic health will be paved with disappointments and new questions, you may find that they will believe you when you have to make an unexpected change. This trust will help stabilize the economy. But tell me, if you didn't know what you were doing, how did you decide to take the often-inconsistent measures that you, and your colleagues finally implemented?

AL. Well, we had experts advising us. Charles had recommended several to me. Some of us followed one set of expert's advice, while others listened to different drummers. I couldn't come up with a coherent policy, partly because the economists that Charles had recommended didn't agree with each other much less with the opposition's "experts".

FATHER. Since when do you listen to Charles?

AL. Well, ...Charles was certain these guys knew which remedies would succeed, and they all held doctorates, and were well known, and... the public trusted them.

FATHER. The people Charles recommended were probably advocates, as well as experts of one sort or another. Experts in economics, as in all other areas of knowledge, have worked hard to develop a preferred theory. Thus they are often advocates for one economic theory or another, and sometimes advocates for one particular pressure group. Plus, economic advisors, experts or not, tell their employers what they already want to hear, or what they think you want to hear. They may try to give you advice that validates an economic plan you've already chosen. They may give you a simple answer for a complex problem that allows you to turn a vague and confused economic notion into a clear but the simple solution that your constituents want. You'd be better off to sit in a quiet room and take time to clearly decide what advice you really believe. Under such circumstances, you may find that you can sometimes develop your own comprehensive solutions by combining the most promising parts of your advisor's suggestions. I must warn you that this process is likely to be neither easy nor foolproof. It requires hard work rather than your usual eyewash and sleight of hand.

AL. If I tried to combine the various points of view provided, I'd be immediately criticized by other 'experts' as leading the country toward ruination or, at best, for not doing enough. We, as legislators, must always appear to be doing enough. Bullshit and sleight of hand are the only things that have reliably saved me and made me as successful as I've been.

FATHER. Did you improve the economy in any way?

AL. (*laughs*) I probably stimulated the economy a little when the economists we hired spent their paychecks. Actually, my colleagues and I don't really know how successful any advice was that we did follow. The people who disagreed with whatever we implemented claimed that the economy would have improved on its own or improved more if we followed different advice, while our experts claimed that the economy would have been much worse if we hadn't followed theirs. Look, the public just wanted a quick and simple path back to prosperity, and all I and most of my colleagues wanted was a quick and simple way to please our electorate. We all ended up disappointed. Instead of simplicity, we advocated competing methods. We tightened here and loosened there. Guiding the economy felt like riding a bicycle on a narrow flat-topped ridge. We would wobble back and forth between opposing disasters. We would inflate the economy because some of our advisors predicted that it would stimulate economic growth. When we approached the edge of hyperinflation, other economists advised us to move to the other, deflation side of the ridge, where eventually total economic depression stared us in the face. The economists said that such wobbling was perfectly normal They called it the business cycle, and said that it was nothing to worry about. The problem with this process was that it felt like little bits of the ridge broke off each time we approached a dangerous edge and then sharply turned away from it. This made the path narrower and narrower. Each time we switched directions we saw ourselves possessing less and less latitude to adjust to the next economic crisis. I'm afraid that eventually there will be no path left for the economy to travel, and we will all tumble into the abyss. To make matters worse, we sometimes changed our minds as telepundits entered the fray, even when it violated whatever overall economic plan we were following at the time. Yes, we ended up zigzagging all over the place as we proposed conflicting legislation and turned a blind eye to its long-term future results. We accomplished a lot less than we could have, because none of us could find a middle ground to follow when every interested party advising us wanted only to support some strongly held economic belief or someone's narrow economic interest that they were hired to represent.

FATHER. A clear and simple path to universal economic health probably does not exist. Our human minds are not big enough to grasp every aspect of an economy. Instead, we have to hack our way through barely predictable and rarely solvable economic challenges to find, at best, temporary economic solutions. You have to accept your limitations and persevere in spite of them. You politicians constantly seem to aim for permanent, conclusive answers. Instead, you should aim for a steadily evolving system. Economic solutions that find a middle path are more likely to survive over a longer period of time. If you work hard enough to understand and map out a middle of the road economic plan you may be able to avoid most garden variety upsets. Slamming on the brakes or pumping like mad as unexpected obstructions rise before you will likely cause even more instability. Ignoring any change in the economy, on the other hand, will also promote the same result. You must respond to these threats, but keep in mind that any radical maneuver is a form of instability itself. Economic solutions can never be final, never be perfect. You have to view your economic remedies not as ends in themselves but as possibly reusable means to accomplish temporary benefits. The search for economic solutions is a race with no end. The history of economics is a history of confusions of ideas. *(Lovejoy) It is the history of trial and error. *(Lovejoy) Even solutions that appear to be clear, coherent, and firmly grounded are unlikely to appear in the eyes of posterity to have any of these attributes. *(Love joy) You must never believe in any proposed economic solution too completely, and always be willing to accept compromise and change when your original plan can't be implemented or no longer works. That is the sum of my advice for whatever it is worth.

AL. I don't see that helping me much. Previously we legislators were pushing economic policy in contrary directions and getting nowhere. Your solution to this chaotic mess allows us to continue to change our minds whenever we want and not have any certainty about where we will end up.

FATHER. No, you shouldn't change your mind whenever you want, but you must be content with a relative and practical understanding, which is the only knowledge we possess. * (Locke) You should change your mind only when you feel you can no longer experience any further progress by following the current path. This change may well involve compromising with colleagues who promote other solutions. Try to maintain a middle course as a baseline rule of thumb while you make your necessary adjustments. A time may come when you must make a revolutionary change to the economy, but never rush into such a situation. Don't have too much faith in your own point of view, when it occurs at the beginning of any new solution or at the end of a previous one that no longer works. My point of view is not that having a point of view is worthless but that you should always be suspicious of any point of view that doesn't move from time to time. I'll try to help you as much as I can, but I can't guarantee you success. In fact, I think the first step you must take will be to simply stop trying to only get re-elected. Once you've given up all hope of prospering from any economic solutions you think up, you'll free yourself to do some really creative thinking.

AL. I'm almost already there, Dad.

FATHER. Then let go. If you do, you will find that your present circumstances offer a little more clarity and certainty than your eventual destination, and more clues about where and how to take your next step. Start out from here. Consider your present understanding of the problem to be a temporary blueprint which you will modify as time passes, but always begin from a position you honestly believe at the time. If from here you move forward with an open mind and a suppressed ego, and you may travel far, though not always to where you expected. I've sometimes said that I don't like where your motivations lead you. Now is your chance to prove me wrong.

AL. (*Looks uncomfortable and then sideways at the Father to see if he is looking at him. He lies.*). OK.

FATHER. Good. Once you see what an impossible job you have ahead of you, you'll be able to understand the economic landscape a lot better. I will help you investigate that landscape.

AL. Wait a minute! If ultimate success is impossible, if I can't hope to succeed either in fixing the economy, or more importantly, uh... in getting elected, why should I bother to do anything?

FATHER. (*Mutters to himself*). "There's no change in him yet, but despair is the last refuge of the ego. When he finally lets go of this ego, he may eventually deserve to be re-elected." (*More loudly to Al*). Ultimate success? Don't chase after such a fantasy. You may, however, locate some temporary successes if you diligently seek them. One of these temporary successes may or may not be your re-election.

AL. Should I hold out any hope at all of succeeding?

FATHER. You must retain hope that you will really accomplish something. You should focus your hopes on this rather than hope to win an election. Traveling hopefully is better than arriving. (Katherine Masefield).

AL. How can I maintain any hope at all if I will always fail in the long run when a solution stops working?

FATHER. Hope can often live quite amicably with lost causes. Hoping for a miracle can be very satisfying and sometimes produces surprising results. Besides, you will never find even a temporary solution to your problems if you lose confidence in your ability to search for something better. Doing nothing leaves everything up to chance, and chance can be a very fickle master. You must develop some confidence, groundless as it may be, in whatever economic solutions you think up. Otherwise, no one will help you test them out. As I'm sure you are aware, you will have to inspire people who have problems tolerating uncertainty. You must inspire hope in them for uncertain solutions with your own honestly held hope, while at the same time, question every step you make. I don't expect you to give up; I only want you to avoid the arrogant attitude that your solutions are the best and only ones, or that the best way to deal with economic problems is to trick people into believing that they don't really exist. I want you to find that uncomfortable but productive state of mind that lies between dogmatic belief and hopelessness, and be honest about where you stand.

AL. I think I can do that. I really don't like giving up. When I have in the past, I've ended up regretting it. For example, I lost a lot of money when I sold out my shares in Charles' company at a loss. It's now doing quite well. Giving up hope certainly didn't serve me very well as an investor.

FATHER. Expectation and hope are two different emotions. You could have expected that the stock would never rise again and still held onto it hoping that it would. Sometimes you can hope that chance will intervene while not changing your expectation that it won't. Expectations of failure shouldn't necessarily prevent you from making reasonable plans of action for success. When you play golf, I doubt that you expect to always make a hole in one. But when you do make that hole in one, it's not due to blind chance alone. You planned for the ball to go in and modified your swing and concentration accordingly. You tried your best to get the ball in the hole, while not expecting to succeed. I'm surprised that you gave up so easily when the stock declined. You've always been a savvy investor.

AL. Yes, I've made a lot of money speculating in the markets. I was always able to bob and weave at just the right time, and then suddenly, I couldn't do it anymore. I don't know how anyone could be so right and then, in an instant, so wrong.

FATHER. That is one of the most important characteristics of economic action. No matter how well an economic measure works in the past, there is no guarantee that it will continue working. There are no permanent economic solutions, no measures that are unimpeachable. There is only uncertainty, and the effort needed to deal with this uncertainty. Effort will be of utmost importance when teasing some kind of meaning out of this uncertainty.

AL. Why is economic uncertainty so intractable?

FATHER. Economic solutions will always remain uncertain because people's attitudes and expectations create the economy as much as mathematics and other objective facts do. Since human attitudes and expectations are often fluid and sometimes unpredictable, the economy also remains unpredictable and murky no matter what measures you take. Managing such an environment can never be perfect or easy. Amy stops by about this time every Wednesday to chat. Unlike you, Priscilla, and Charles, she visits me a lot, and she often talks about the same concerns that I believe many of your other constituents also have. I'll call her up and see if she can come over to help you understand what she wants and expects from the economy.

AL. It's easy for Amy to find time to stop in. She has a lot of time on her hands, (*Al looks down at his own hands*), since her school district cut her position along with a number of others.

FATHER. She ought to provide you with a useful perspective then. Priscilla called me earlier and for some reason wants to talk to me. Why don't I call Charles and ask him to come over too? It's been a long time since we've had a family reunion, and perhaps we can mine their thoughts to determine what economic or other measures you could take that would benefit the most people.

AL. That's not a good idea. None of them are talking to me right now. Each thinks I have betrayed their trust.

FATHER. (*Gets up and leaves for the other room to make his phone call*).

FATHER. (*Calls from the other room*). And have they reason to be dissatisfied with you?

AL. (*Shouts back*). It's not my fault. I tried to make everyone happy! People like Charles said their taxes were too high. So I submitted a bill to cut taxes and didn't have enough money to fund education, which forced the schools to lay off teachers. Now Amy hates me and claims I was unfair, and Charles claims that I haven't lowered his taxes enough. And Priscilla, well, we both know there is no pleasing her. (Sits quietly feeling sorry for himself).

FATHER. (*Reenters the room*). You weren't a leader, but a herky-jerky follower. You've reacted like a puppet on a string to whoever wanted something from you. I'm surprised in you. I thought you liked to call the shots.

AL. I do, but I've learned that I can't lead a large group of people somewhere they don't already want to go. Your thoughts about advisors support this fundamental truth.

FATHER. You're supposed to lead, and represent, and advise. Rather than follow and support everything your unruly constituents want you to do, you sometimes need to persuade them to follow what you believe is the best path. A true leader may need to persuade people to go places they never thought of going in the first place.

AL. First of all, as I keep telling you, I don't know where to go. Secondly, the individual members of the public are often so antagonistic toward each other that many will view anything I do with suspicion. Some will even view my efforts as collusion with their enemies.

FATHER. It sounds like you've lost sight of the many options that life presents to you.

AL. I once thought I could access all this potential you think lies waiting for me to tap. Experience has taught me otherwise.

FATHER. While you shouldn't make demands with which the public can't cope, or that contradict human nature, *(Adam Phillips) most people can be persuaded to follow an economic program if you can demonstrate that you will use your power in a fair and honorable manner that honestly tries to improve economic conditions for as many of your constituents as possible.

AL. So I should just ignore everyone and do whatever feels right?

FATHER. Given that you don't seem to have any clue about what to do next, I'd recommend that you continue to listen to as many opinions as possible, but don't put all of your faith in everything they tell you. Always be suspicious of any point of view that doesn't move from time to time, or doesn't leave a way for you to reverse yourself if it begins to look like a mistake. Never relax by thinking that you completely understand the problem or its solution. If you hit a dead end, start over again. No matter how frustrating the process, continue to believe that you can eventually reach some sort of answer. Find solutions via the traditional method of "acertare errado", by ascertaining through error. After acting, step back from what you've done to better view it objectively, then step back in if you need to take further steps. Action without thought and thought without action can't bring you much success. Biased parties will try to persuade you to continue to press on even when you recognize that your solution isn't working or is pushing you close to the edge of a new problem. "Double down" they will suggest, or "Don't turn back". Think first and consult competing points of view before taking such advice.

AL. But I've often found that it only takes one last push to succeed at something that has been resisting me. You've always told me not to give up.

FATHER. I'm not advising you to give up, just to be flexible. Change is the only certainty that I can locate in economics, and it is best you learn to accept that now. Sooner or later, your remedies will stop working, and you need to be prepared to advance new, well-considered ones. Don't worry about looking inconsistent. A good leader exhibits <u>both</u> versatility and consistency during times of tribulation. * (Ian F McNealy) Try one thing, then another, and another, but always put your full faith and effort behind each attempt. You must honestly believe that every solution you promote will work, but be willing to immediately let go of this belief when it no longer does. Yes, you might wobble from side to side a bit when guiding the economy, but try the best you can to steer a stable course by never taking your eye off of the middle ground. Try to stay away from the edges of disaster by not making the same mistakes over and over again. Some may propose solutions that you cannot reverse, or escape from. Avoid such all or nothing traps. They may even seek to destroy other options you have before you can use them in order to ensure that you will follow only their pet theories. Beware of such advisors. By all means listen, but don't trust everything you hear. Consider it all, and then make up your own mind and use your well-considered ideas when you finally choose to act.

LES MISERABLES?

(*A woman in her early thirties enters the room. Her hair is disheveled, but she is smiling until she sees Al. She then bursts into tears*).

AL. (*Looks at her thoughtfully and a bit sadly then brightens up*). Hey Amy you're looking as beautiful as ever!

FATHER. (*Takes a sharp look at Al*). Amy, are you all right?

AMY. (*sniffs*) No, I'm not all right. Al and his friends cut the money for my school and since my school didn't have the money to pay three third grade teachers, and since I have the least seniority, the school laid me off. (*She turns to Al, and blows her nose*) You did this to me! That teaching job was my life. Why would you take it from me? I thought we were friends. And I'm not the only one to suffer; the remaining two teachers each have to teach forty third graders. Do you know how difficult that will be? Miss Prince will celebrate her sixtieth birthday next month, and she can't get around as well as when she was younger. She can't possibly control forty children in one classroom; much less provide the special help that some of the students need.

AL. I'm truly sorry Amy, but we just didn't have the money anymore. Tax revenue had shrunk and the cost of keeping the unemployed clothed and fed rose. We had to cut somewhere. You wouldn't want to see people go cold and hungry, would you?

AMY. (*Sniffs and shakes her head 'no'*).

AL. I didn't want to vote for the cuts, but keeping people alive trumps educating them, …don't you think? You receive unemployment benefits don't you? Would you rather that I voted to cut those benefits instead?

AMY. But if you kept that money in the schools I wouldn't need…

AL. (*Quickly interjects*) or cut the benefits for some of your student's parents?

AMY. (*Sighs in resignation*) No. I just don't understand why we need to cut spending anywhere. If we all share fairly, there must be enough money to keep everyone happy. In this country a lot of people have a lot of money. Someone must not be sharing. Why didn't you pass a law to make everyone share Al?

AL. It's not called sharing unless people want to share. I don't think that people will consider it sharing if I pass a law making them do so. Instead of experiencing your warm fuzzy feeling of sharing they will likely experience something much more unpleasant.

AMY. Maybe so, but, do something good for a change. You've done nothing but hurt all our schools, our students and…. all of us. You've become heartless and evil. No wonder Priscilla hates you!

AL. You know that I'm not as bad as Priscilla says I am. I want to do the right thing. What would you have me do, Amy?

AMY. Put the funds we need back into the education budget.

AL. Whose money do you want me to take to do this?

AMY. I don't want you to <u>take</u> anyone's money. Can't you just convince people to give more? Maybe you can persuade the people with money to donate some of it to the schools.

FATHER. (*Looks at Al with expectation*)

AL. (*Looks at Amy with bemused amazement. He shakes his head "no" while unsuccessfully suppressing a smile.*)

FATHER. (*Looks over at Al with his own, much sadder look of amazement*). Surely there is something you could try to do. It's not like you to give up so completely.

AL. I haven't given up. Give me some new ideas, and I'll implement them. Persuading the rich to voluntarily give some of their wealth to good causes is as old as the hills, and it never makes up for a government's lack of money. I can't build a permanent dam to hold back what has become a rising tide of economic disaster with old tools that can't handle the job. I need new tools. So far, neither you nor Amy has given me anything I can really use. Perhaps I need to look elsewhere for an answer.

AMY. (*Grins*) Maybe your answer just walked into the door.

(*A tall severe looking woman walks into the room. Her posture is as stiff and straight as a board*).

PRISCILLA. (*Glares at Al then glances over to her father*). Trying to help this unregenerate sinner again father with some vague and ungodly advice? There should certainly be a better use of your time if you ask me. (*Turns to Al*). You need more than a few of Father's ideas to redeem yourself and rise above the unholy mess you've created. You need to develop a better character, more honesty, and a strong faith in God before a sinner like you can set anything right. A rather unlikely development, I fear.

AL. (*impatiently sighs*) Hello Priscilla. Still angry about the government loan I procured for Charles's stem cell research company?

PRISCILLA. You've compounded your sins since then. I lay all the suffering my flock has endured over the past year on you and your friends in Congress who coddle the decadently wealthy while ignoring the suffering of the poor. Yes I'm still angry with you for facilitating that loan to Charles, and even more for investing some of your own money in his business. You swore to me before almighty God that you opposed the project. You flat out lied. I believe you to be more evil than even that godless sinner Charles who worships only science and what he calls "facts". At least he has enough character to honestly state what he believes and what he intends, as demonic and soulless as it is. You, on the other hand, lie, distort and manipulate everything and everyone. You believe in nothing and support evil if you think you can benefit from it. You deserve to be thrown into the lowest reaches of hell! And I blame you father, for Al's lack of respect for the truth. After all, you are always trying to persuade us that uncertainty possesses some sort of positive value. You teach that truths are mutable, and that if someone does not like a fact that someone else has constructed, we can construct another fact that we prefer. In fact, your philosophy possesses no value at all. It only undermines and dissolves the reality of any truth; a philosophy that serves Al's self-serving ends quite nicely.

FATHER. Priscilla, I just accept that some "facts" are not facts at all. Some are instead socially determined beliefs. That includes not only some economic "facts" as well as many of your religious tenets. Probably nothing we think or believe can be eternally true, because reality constantly changes around us, and we change with it. What may have been true yesterday is no longer true today.

PRISCILLA. There are some facts that cannot be challenged. If you challenge the existence of these facts you challenge the existence of truth itself.

FATHER. You misunderstand my philosophy Priscilla. I value the truth as much as you do. I just don't believe we can ever know it completely. A partial truth can be valuable and useful, as long as we continue to look for other, hidden aspects of this truth as our situation changes.

PRISCILLA. There is only one truth. Everything else is falsehood.

AL. What truth is that?

PRISCILLA. God's truth. He has laid it out before us as clear as day. The problem is that none of you choose to see it.

AMY. (Squirms uncomfortably in her chair).

AL. (*Rolls his eyes*).

FATHER. This truth you speak of doesn't seem to me to be clear at all. Everyone seems to disagree about what God's truth really is. I've even heard you contradict yourself sometimes. In my case, I believe in a mysterious order to the universe, which we mold with our emotions and intellect into our personal understanding of God. I find this belief spiritually fulfilling, but not absolutely true. There may be other truths about God that I just cannot see or understand.

PRISCILLA. Clearly you see and understand nothing. The truth can be found only in the teachings of Jesus Christ.

FATHER. What brings you here today Priscilla? Come to convert me?

PRISCILLA. I have been having second thoughts about turning down the financial part of your legacy. Due to the economic collapse caused by this one (points at Al), donations have dropped off significantly to my church, its food pantry and to the missionary efforts I support. I'd like to see if there is some way I might qualify for your legacy after all.

AMY. I didn't come here for the legacy, but I do need a short-term loan, Daddy. Don't worry; I'll pay you back as soon as I find a job.

PRISCILLA. Idle hands do the devil's work, Amy. You need to take care.

(*A tall, neatly dressed, bespectacled man enters the room and immediately begins to glare at Priscilla*).

CHARLES. Rabidly spouting your idiotic superstitions again Priscilla? I was rather hoping that I wouldn't run into you here today. (*Looks over at Amy*). Since unemployment has risen steadily and all the schools are terminating teachers, I'd think twice about that loan to Amy Father. She won't be paying you back anytime soon. She's definitely a bad credit risk. (*He sits down confidently.*) I, on the other hand, I am sitting on the cusp of another scientific breakthrough. Since Al sold all the stock he held my company, (*Priscilla looks over at Al and smiles*), and I need fresh investors to move my new project forward. I have, of course, gained quite a bit of capital from the sale of my stem cell research patents, but it won't be enough to fund my new project, and so I too am interested in picking up a bit of the cash portion of your legacy. (*Looks over at Al*). Sorry Al, there was money to be made from that stem cell research but you were you were too foolish and impatient to wait around for the <u>big</u> payday. If you possessed a more rational, scientifically oriented mind you could have seen that my research would eventually turn profitable. (*Turns to his father*) I know that you father, unlike Priscilla, realize that science ultimately benefits everyone. You could make money and at the same time benefit humanity by replacing Al's investment in my new project. If you don't want to personally invest, perhaps a share of the legacy would do the trick.

FATHER. I don't like the word "ultimately". We never live long enough to see the final results of anything. Are you willing to accept the rest of the legacy? Are you willing to accept the uncertainty of reason, objectivity, and scientific

CHARLES. (Snorts.) Hardly.

PRISCILLA. (*Puffing herself up a bit*). So Al, you finally recognized the sinful nature of Charles' attempts to pervert God's plan by manipulating stem cells.

AL. It was sinful all right. (*Mumbles*), "Losing money always feels like a sin". (*Speaks louder*), Charles project was destined for failure.

CHARLES. You've always possessed accurate insights about Al, father. I should have seen what you've always seen. He's a lying, deceitful, manipulative politician. He's never really believed in either science or me. He's never shown any commitment to the truth. He believes in nothing but himself.

AL. Others doubt your new project as much as I do. A reliable source told me that the Economic Development Council will soon call in your government loan. Those patents you sold aren't producing any income for the buyers, and the Council believes your new project is just too speculative.

CHARLES. What! I'll bet that you had something to do with the recall of the loan. You're despicable! (*Al crosses his arms and begins to shake his head "no", while Priscilla shakes her head confidently "yes"*). Father I apparently need your help now more than ever. Can I count on your support?

FATHER. As an investor? No. But perhaps you will learn how to become a better heir to my legacy if you remain here for the afternoon. It's still possible, you know, though your certainty about all things seems to disqualify you at this point. Since economics seems to be on everyone's mind today, let's spend the afternoon discussing the uncertainties of economics and how we can act in the face of these uncertainties. Maybe we can help each other address the economic problems that Al and perhaps each of you have helped create.

AL. (*A bit humble at last*) I'd appreciate that. The public has turned against me, and as a result, I can't accomplish anything. My constituents won't consider anything I propose, and I expect to be out of office after the next election.

FATHER. (*Nods and smiles at Al*).

CHARLES. You earned your own disgrace when you seeded, cultivated, and fertilized your supporter's emotions. Now you harvest their raw unreason that you cannot channel or manipulate in any way. Better if you had chosen to cultivate reason as I do. If you had trained your supporters to embrace logic and reason they would always recognize and support the correct economic solutions.

FATHER. Why is that?

CHARLES. Because reason always leads to the truth.

FATHER. Not necessarily, and it sometimes creates even more intractable problems than the ones you set out to solve.

CHARLES. Piffle!

PRISCILLA. Economics emits a stench of worldly sin that often worms its way into our immortal souls in the form of greed. I find such a discussion distasteful, but will stay and listen in order to confront and defeat this sin and clear a path to Almighty God for you sinners. (*She looks directly at Amy*).

FATHER. I value your willingness to stay as well as, hopefully, your promise to listen.

CHARLES. Ah, economics. While it doesn't possess purely scientific credentials, it is a discipline based on reason. Actually, I know quite a bit about economics.

AMY. (*Groans*). Is there anything you don't know about?

CHARLES. I took several Economics courses in college. I think I'm going to like this discussion. I'll certainly like it more than the last discussion we had about religion. I think I'll serve as a great resource for you, father, in explaining economic facts. I don't understand, however, why you want Priscilla to remain. She's a religious fanatic who believes her god has a hand in everything. She knows absolutely nothing about economics, and can bring nothing to any discussion about it.

FATHER. Maybe she can. Faith seems to underlie all aspects of economics, whether it is faith in government, faith in eternal economic growth, faith in economic laws, or faith that economies operate with the precision and rationality of a machine. Priscilla seems to know a lot about faith. She might fit right in.

CHARLES. Nonsense!

AL. (*Looks relieved that the group's focus is off him for the moment*).

FATHER. Our relationship with economics is a bit like our relationship with god and religion. We can never be absolutely certain we perceive and understand economics correctly. We can't know when we have found the best possible economic system possible. We can't even be certain that a perfect system can exist. We can only make economic choices based on a shifting combination of faith, reason, and emotion.

AMY. I'll stay to listen too. I just enjoy being here with my family, and I'm always ready to listen to you Daddy, even if I don't fully understand what you are talking about.

ORTHODOXY OR HERESY?

FATHER. I suspect that each of you, whether you know it or not, follows a belief in one type of economic system over another. I'm curious which system you think would work best for you and why you think it would. If one system answers all our needs, than the answers to our economic dilemmas should be simple. We should simply follow the dictates of the economic system we all agree is best for us, though I think you will find such agreement a lot more difficult than you expect.

CHARLES. Nonsense! Capitalism has certainly proven itself superior to all previous and all currently competing systems. I'm confident that it is the only system that can possibly solve all of our current economic problems.

AL. I'm with you all the way, brother!

FATHER. You have full faith in capitalism, Charles, although it allowed Al to suddenly sell his shares in your company and by doing so weakened its worth and financial stability of your company? Doesn't that bother you?

AL. (*Wanting to short circuit any discussion that leads back to him*). Yes Charles, we've always agreed that capitalism is the only economic system that supports quick, substantial economic growth. What my constituents, and I need is another mighty spurt of economic growth, and we need it right now! (*He nods and smiles at Charles as though they are natural allies*).

CHARLES. (*Scowls angrily at Al*).

AMY. The only benefit I can see in this capitalism you two are always cheering about is that it gives people like you who are only capable of thinking about your own well-being permission to play your selfish games. It has done nothing for me.

PRISCILLA. Nor my flock and me.

FATHER. Capitalism can also produce immediate and massive economic contractions, Charles. Why aren't you afraid that capitalism, if left to its own devices, will make your current situation worse instead of better?

AL. (*Speaks with false bravado*). We're more than willing to take that chance, aren't we Charles. I always say nothing ventured nothing....well you know. In order for me to do anything I have to take that leap of faith you, Father and Priscilla are always talking about. Right now capitalism appears to offer the only hope for a quick and effective removal of the pain we are **all** experiencing. (*He looks around the room at the others*). I know about the risks embedded in our current economic system, but no other system offers this kind of hope. Right?

CHARLES. Yes, as a politician, hope provides the only currency you have to buy the public's support and acceptance right now. Too bad you can't offer anything more substantial that you could marinate with your so-called hope.

AL. (*Al bites his lip and says nothing*).

FATHER. Priscilla, what economic system do you feel provides the most hope for humanity?

PRISCILLA. None of them provide any hope at all. Like planets revolving around the sun, something that Charles claims to understand, all economic systems revolve around money and the material baubles that money can buy. The difference is that such material things cast off no light, no understanding and no hope. Money is the root of all evil. It nourishes human greed, egotism, and decadent lifestyles. (She glances over at Amy and) It encourages the manipulation and oppression of one group of people by another. It supports the whole corrosive concept of winners and losers. I believe, father, that the last time we met you agreed that dividing humankind into winners and losers caused a great deal of suffering and unhappiness for those living under Roman rule. I, for one, know that a perfect system for human well-being and happiness exists only under the immaterial economics of the Kingdom of God.

FATHER. What could this economic system possibly resemble?

PRISCILLA. God will see to everyone's needs, with no one getting more than they deserve. Everyone would share the available resources, and treat each other with kindness and charity.

AMY. I like the sound of that.

CHARLES. In other words each would provide to the community according to his abilities, and each would receive according to his needs.

PRISCILLA. Yes. That kind of fairness would prevail.

CHARLES. Your economic system of the Kingdom of God is communism pure and simple. The powers at the top supposedly provide for all the needs of the followers at the bottom, who work just for the hell of it. I admit that people probably don't have to work too hard in your imaginary system. Their most difficult task would be to believe in the omniscience and omnipotence of God, and his authority. Come to think of it, that sounds like the communist system too. (*He chuckles*.). The only difference between the two is that communists don't believe in God, probably because they see your Kingdom of God as a similar competing entity to the Communist state and its central, absolute authority.

PRISCILLA. No, communist materialism has no role in heaven or the Kingdom of God. Communism attempts to address only people's material needs. People have no material needs in heaven, and only the most basic needs here on earth when they accept God's safekeeping. People should never need fancy food, luxurious dwellings, the latest fashions, or novel amusements on earth or in heaven. They need none of these things. They need only freedom from wanting these things. These superficial wants will be replaced by a fullness of happiness that springs from their closeness to God.

AMY. Heaven and the Kingdom of God sound pretty dull. I've changed my mind about it.

AL. People are supposed to want to enter the Kingdom of God, right?

PRISCILLA. Of course, why do you ask?

AL. I think the only people who would want to go there are people who see no joy in this world, and want nothing more than escape it. (*Amy nods in agreement*). This was probably true about the people who chose to follow communism.

FATHER. Priscilla, do you have any thoughts about economic life as it currently exists in this world?

PRISCILLA. (*Thinks a moment*). I believe in the value of work. It builds character, and as such is a godly activity. It prepares people for entry into the Kingdom of God. While I don't consider believing in the authority of God to be the onerous work that Charles thinks it is, daily work does require a similar involvement of mental and emotional discipline that a belief in God requires. Holding down a job here on earth brings us one step closer to experiencing the Kingdom of God. We mustn't see work so much as a way to acquire money but rather as a way to acquire God's grace and love. So, yes, I believe that full employment should be encouraged here on earth, and idleness punished as long as the work adheres to moral and religious correctness and holds the approval of the Highest Authority.

AL. I certainly believe in full employment! (*Priscilla glances over at him in disgust*).

CHARLES. Just as I thought. She's a radical communist.

FATHER. (*Ignoring Charles*). Amy, if you had a choice, what economic system would you choose?

AMY. I don't know much about the difference between this and communism or any other "ism". I just know that I would rather live in a world where everyone shared what he or she has because they want to share; because they enjoy sharing, and not because some "authority" makes them do it. If you have money, you should want to share it with those who don't. If you possess useful ideas or special knowledge you should use it to help others, and not to take advantage of them. If you have spare time, you should also use it to help people who need attention. If we would all follow this approach we would have what we need and live happily ever after. I know you say that heaven is a pleasant place Priscilla, but I would rather be happy in this world loving the people you consider flawed who I already know. People have material needs, Priscilla, as well as spiritual ones. I can't be happy if I can't taste and touch and see and hear the good things this world can provide if we would only work together to create them. Money is very useful in providing these things and I don't see how amassing money or even money itself is evil if we are all willing to share it once we have it.

AL. Exactly! I've always supported people sharing their wealth.

FATHER. How?

AL. Uh.....through taxes? (Priscilla smirks, and Amy looks dumbfounded).

CHARLES. Amy you sound a bit like a socialist, though people don't really volunteer to give up their money under socialism. Socialism doesn't encourage sharing. It mandates it, and that makes all the difference in the world. People don't really look out for each other under Socialism, because they figure the government will do it for them. More real charity and sympathy occurs under socialism. Socialism's forced sharing often causes a backlash. Those whom the government forces to share through taxation end up hiding their excess wealth rather than giving it away.

AMY. You **would** say that.

AL. I'm not so sure that taxation causes people to be less charitable, Charles. Those people who would rather hide their wealth probably wouldn't have done much to help the less fortunate anyway, no matter what their taxes were.

FATHER. People do volunteer to live in socialist economic systems, Charles, when they vote in Socialist governments.

CHARLES. I don't see anyone getting wealthy in an economy where everyone shares.

PRISCILLA. That's the point.

AMY. If we all have nice clothes, and yummy foods, and nice places to live, aren't we all wealthy? If we're all busy helping each other, aren't we all employed?

CHARLES. There's no real incentive to promote economic growth in an economy where everything is shared. Who retains enough capital to fund the machinery and stores and lumber yards and iron mines to create all this comfort? Not all wealth can be shared. Some needs to be gathered and plowed back into the businesses that provide all these things. Without the economic growth that amassed capital investment can provide, everyone will end up poor, not rich Amy. People will have no hope for the future when there is no possibility for economic growth.

PRISCILLA. We don't need eternal economic growth. We don't need to become wealthy to be free and live a blessed life.

FATHER. What do we need then?

PRISCILLA. We need to embrace the infinite fullness of God.

(*Al and Amy look at each other in amazement*).

CHARLES. Good luck with that.

AMY. Economic growth? There will always be economic growth, won't there? People will have babies and will work to provide for their children. This work will create new wealth that can be shared. Right? People can pool their money to buy the equipment needed to do this work. That is a form of sharing. And when their children grow up, they will work and take care of their parents just as their parents took care of them. Since the population will keep growing, the economy will keep growing. There will be plenty of hope and happiness to go around. There will be more money moving around and more people helping each other as time passes.

FATHER. She's right in that economic growth can occur without concentrating wealth in the hands of a few capitalists. Socialist societies similar to Amy's, uh, Kingdom of Sharing (*He smiles at Amy and she smiles back*), have sometimes exhibited solid economic growth, just not the explosive growth of capitalist societies.

AL. As Charles pointed out; Amy's economy really isn't a socialist one. In her economy people volunteer to help their "friends", while under socialism, the government takes a substantial share of the wealth and invests in state run industries and services. The government makes people share with other people and businesses that they don't know and might not even like.

FATHER. This is true, but the broad intent of each system is the same. Like Amy's economic system, socialism expects the group to take care of its members. It just doesn't possess the same trust in human nature that Amy does.

CHARLES. (*Smugly glances over at Amy*). Well Amy, your willingness to share will soon be tested. Your unemployment insurance benefits will soon run out. Are you really happy that you will receive less income so that the government can hire more people to fix the roads and bridges that are in need of repair? As I recall, you don't own a car do you? In a sense you are already sharing your wealth and lowering your standard of living so that things you don't even care about can be accomplished, and so that others can improve their wealth and standard of living while yours is declining. How does that make you feel? This is socialism, or at least the socialism with which we've watered down our capitalistic economy. I know this socialist infection of capitalism hasn't helped me one whit, and it won't help you much either. You'll get by, but that's about all., capitalism on the other hand has done everything for me. It has allowed me to acquire quite a bit of wealth over a short period of time. It has made me much happier than either you or I could ever be under your system. I'm even happier than we would be if your Socialist economy somehow did manage to meet all of its objectives without confiscating any of my wealth, because under Socialism I would have little hope of ever becoming really wealthy, and I find that idea extremely depressing. A material girl like yourself wouldn't taste or touch as many nice things under socialism as you might under a purely capitalist economy. You wouldn't like the mediocre standard of living that socialism would, at best, be able to provide.

PRISCILLA. As usual you are blind to the truth staring you in the face. The greed fostered by capitalism destroyed the economy and made Amy poor, not socialism.

AL. Priscilla is onto something here Charles. Amy was laid off because the government couldn't collect enough tax revenue to pay her. Tax revenue was low because the economy went into the tank. The economy fell apart because the stock market collapsed, and the stock market fell apart because capitalists like you got greedy and started speculating on risky investments in order to make more and more money more and more quickly. The socialist infection you worry about had nothing to do with it. In fact, unemployment insurance, one of the socialist aspects of our current capitalist economy is probably one of the only economic devices that will temporarily keep her head above water. Under the pure capitalism that you so esteem someone like Amy probably wouldn't survive at all. Government is doing its job here.

PRISCILLA. I'm sure Amy would survive quite nicely. (*She throws a piercing stare in Amy's direction, which she coldly ignores*).

AMY. I would survive because unlike you Charlie, I have friends who would help me out if I ran out of money and need something to taste or touch. These friendships would provide me with a happiness that more than makes up for any discomfort my reduced wealth may cause. I would help them in return. I would baby-sit for them, and make cookies for them just as I already do. The only thing I would really miss is the job itself. I loved my job. I enjoyed teaching children the skills they will need to live a good life. I enjoyed dealing with my coworkers. I felt truly needed. That's what I will miss, not the money.

AL. (*Al looks at her with sincere sadness*). I'm afraid you will start to miss the money soon enough if I don't find some other way to help you.

PRISCILLA. Rather than rely on friends and unemployment insurance for your economic support, you should just go out and take a job. Any real job. The unpaid services you propose to do for your friends aren't really work at all. It's just a useful form of idleness. I fear you will be tempted into sin by this idleness. You need a real job that builds character rather than one you do for fun. I recommend that you take a job that imposes some sort of discipline and effort on your part, no matter what it pays.

FATHER. You don't think that Amy's helping her friends builds character.

PRISCILLA. No, it's too easy for her. There's no effort to justify the help she will receive.

(*Under her breath*) And she relies too much on her men friends for her support.

FATHER. Charles you claim to know a lot about economics. How have other economic systems measured up to capitalism over the course of time?

CHARLES. While no other economic system has provided all the benefits that capitalism has provided, some do offer a few benefits that capitalism cannot.

FATHER. (*Looks at Charles with a mixture of admiration and amazement*). You admit then that capitalism isn't a perfect economic system?

CHARLES. It's the best of the bunch. As I said earlier it stimulates economic growth better than any other system and uses available resources such as labor and capital in the most efficient ways possible. Perhaps it doesn't distribute wealth particularly fairly and evenly among its participants, I'll grant you that, but this seems to me to be a small price to pay for long-term economic growth. The only practical answer to our country's economic problems Al, is to grow our way out of them by utilizing all the benefits of capitalism.

FATHER. We have a capitalist system now, and we are not growing our way out of our problems. Some of them seem worse than ever.

CHARLES. Such as?

AL. Such as more a more people in the middle class, people with good educations, like Amy, (He nods and smiles at Amy), no longer have jobs and have fallen onto hard times. Rather than guarantee the efficient use of resources that you claim capitalism provides, we can see right here in this room how it wastes resources. Capitalism is not efficiently using Amy's talents is it? And you're struggling to raise capital for your new project aren't you? Skills and capital lie idle because no capitalist thinks he can make a quick buck from them.

CHARLES. If investors understood my new project correctly they would realize that I could make them very wealthy. And Amy? Well I don't… (*He trails off*). Look, the real reason capitalism isn't solving our economic problems Al, is that you in the government won't let it operate freely. You constantly hamstring it with regulations and restrictions. Government needs to step out of the way of capitalism and let it run free! You'd be surprised how quickly our economic problems would solve themselves if the government would fold up its tents, depart the battle, and leave the economy to us business people.

PRISCILLA. By all means Al, make it happen! Release an economy of untrammeled greed and godless materialism from its government chains! Giving capitalism free rein will only make my long awaited "End of Days" arrive sooner. I want to see fire and brimstone engulf all the dirty business of this world as soon as possible.

FATHER. While I don't believe that destroying the world and all of its economic activity is a viable solution to our problems, I can understand why you are frustrated with the moral emptiness and manic scramble for money that now dominates so much of modern economic life. Giving free rein to capitalism would indeed encourage these unwelcome fellow travelers. Capitalism 's tendency to squeeze daily life into a profit based straight jacket feels very wrong and sick, I agree, but the solution to this problem should not be to destroy the patient in order to destroy the disease.

AL. Perhaps we can solve most of 's problems simply through better management. We don't have to destroy anything. We just need to suppress 's weaknesses while nurturing its strengths. Someone needs to manage the economic growth capitalism can provide so that the positive curve of the business cycle lasts as long as possible. I don't think that those participants of the Capitalist economy who scramble about trying to make money as fast as they can make the wisest managers. Advocates of pure capitalism such as Charles think that capitalism manages itself. This is not true, and if Charles were honest with himself, he would admit as much, since he would never manage his own business by letting it take care of itself. Government is in the best position to manage capitalism wisely and fairly. The economy needs a referee. You can't let the players manage the game; otherwise there would be nothing but constant fighting.

(*Priscilla raises her eyebrows, Amy barks out a cough and Charles laughs out loud*).

CHARLES. I'd rather have no referee than one like you who often has money in the game.

FATHER. You should have thought about that before you brought Al in as a partner. But you make a valid point. Capitalism 's susceptibility to corruption forms another of its weaknesses.

CHARLES. Corruption is not an issue in an economy where the only rule is the survival of the fittest. Without a referee to restrain business only the best and fittest businesses would survive, and their fast growth would pull the overall economy's growth along with them.

AL. Not necessarily. Sometimes the most brutal businesses repress economic growth rather than stimulate it.

CHARLES. Wherever Walmart shows up, it crushes the local mom and pop stores, and as a result consumers receive cheaper prices, and a greater selection of goods More goods are bought and sold. Walmart wins. Walmart's suppliers win. The consumer wins. Everyone wins.

AL. Mom and pop don't win.

FATHER. Nor do some of the Walmart's suppliers.

AMY. I don't like the violence you describe. Why does anyone have to be crushed?

CHARLES. Business is much like war.

AMY. It shouldn't be. A lot of innocent people get hurt in wars. A good economy should avoid conflict. It should promote peace and stability.

AL. She's right, Charles. Most business people want a stable economy, and not one constantly going through changes. Businesses need stability to make long-term plans, to establish trading partners, and to develop markets. Business wars, like real wars can leave an economy in tatters.

CHARLES. Once the business wars have sorted out the winners and losers, peace and stability reintroduces itself.

FATHER. I see. Like Tacitus's observation about the Romans "you propose to ravage, to slaughter, to usurp under false titles, and call it empire; and where you make a desert, you will call it peace."

CHARLES. What's wrong with that. The Romans built a great empire didn't they? Their economy was stronger and more stable than any of their neighbors. We could do worse than copy the Romans.

PRISCILLA. They crucified the Son of God. What is worse than that?

AMY. You're starting to scare me Charles.

AL. All that's left of that great Roman economy Charles are broken stones. I think Amy's economy of co-operation possesses more durability.

CHARLES. (*Laughs bitterly*) Campaigning again I see. Do you really think you and your government pals can build a stronger and more long lasting economy than the Romans could?

AL. Yes, because we have to. Isn't that right Father?

FATHER. You have to believe you can.

CHARLES. (*Shakes his head in disbelief*).

FATHER. Capitalism does some things well, but not everything. The same can be said for socialism. You might find that combining the two works even better than each operating on their own.

CHARLES. Nonsense! I have seen for myself that capitalism promotes economic growth while socialism does not. Former socialist countries like Great Britain have wisely chosen to move away from socialism toward more capitalistic economic solutions. They have benefited as a result. When China restructured its economy from a communist to a capitalist one, its economic growth exploded, and it has become the world's second largest economy. It has become the beacon of hope for the continuation of world wide economic growth. In light of this evidence, how can you even consider watering down 's success with even a tiny drop of socialism's sloth and failure?

AMY. And yet we're all sitting here in this room, each of us finding ourselves in some sort of trouble caused by capitalist economics. I'm unemployed. Your business can't find investors. Priscilla's food pantry is empty, and you Al, may soon be standing next to me on the unemployment line. Take it from me Al; it really hurts to be seen as a loser.

CHARLES. Capitalism can recharge this economy a lot faster than your idealistic ramblings about sharing can Amy. Your socialism might allow this dying economy to linger a bit longer, choking and gasping for breath, but it will die, never-the-less. Best to put it out of its misery.

FATHER. (*Trying to divert an argument*). All economies and economic transactions are more complicated and involve hidden factors not included in your simplistic survival of the fittest philosophy. Charles. I'm not sure that China makes an acceptable example of capitalist competition. Yes, individual investors have poured capital into building new factories, and more efficient technologies. These factories fulfill existing demand for cheaper and better quality products, but the Chinese economy is not the capitalistic free market you think it is. The government still controls the economy. It pressures banks to invest in some businesses and not in others. It plays a role in determining where the investors will build their factories. It determines when and where infrastructure projects will be built. It controls the value of the economy's currency, and conducts a foreign policy that helps its businesses access raw materials. Are you sure that only the advantages of 's free markets have made China's economy so powerful? Might there be a few very uncapitalistic factors at work here?

AL. Such as?

FATHER. Cheap labor, cheap credit, and a good dollop of central planning.

CHARLES. The first two are also factors in a capitalist economy. When either becomes too expensive an economic contraction soon adjusts these factors if the government will allow it.

FATHER. Government intervention in helping private businesses acquire the raw materials they need doesn't sound very capitalistic. Neither does government influence over whom private lending nor the government manipulation of its currency.

AMY. Has capitalism helped the poor people of China?

FATHER. It has created a lot more wealth, many people have become very wealthy, and yes, the general standard of living of the country has improved, but the greatest part of this new wealth has flowed into the hands of a small group of people.

CHARLES. It's only natural that this will occur. It will always occur sooner or later no matter what economic system you have in place. The capitalists who acquire this wealth reinvest it into new businesses that create additional wealth for themselves and new jobs for others. This concentrated wealth has a positive effect on the entire economy and on the economic health of the country as a whole.

FATHER. They sometimes use their profits to purchase machinery that replaces workers, and they don't always reinvest it. Sometimes they just throw it away on a lavish lifestyle.

CHARLES. This spending helps the economy too and others too. People will be employed to make the machines, and provide for the capitalist's spare time needs.

AL. (*Thinking*). Not as much as investing it in new businesses or directly hiring more workers would.

FATHER. When they do invest in new or expanded businesses, as they have in China, the new jobs often pay very little, and most of the new wealth created continues to flow unevenly into the hands of a minority. Socialism may create wealth much more slowly, because it distributes more of the wealth generated by businesses to a broad cross section of its citizens, and this leaves less for reinvestment, but the gap between the richest and the poorest remains reasonable, and a greater proportion of the population enjoys a comfortable standard of living. Everyone has his or her basic needs fulfilled. Socialism provides cheap healthcare, education, and affordable housing for the majority of an economy's members. provides these benefits and much more to the most successful but less to everyone else, and much less to the unemployed and underemployed. People Charles would call the losers. helps individuals while socialism helps the group as a whole.

CHARLES. If the government is going to take care of the least successful no matter how little they contribute to the economy, why would anyone invest, take risks, or even try to succeed at all? Most people would be happy just to get by.

PRISCILLA. Yes, socialism encourages sloth. People who will not work, should not be rewarded, or enjoy life. When people refuse to work...if they would rather sin than work, (*She looks at Amy*), they should be punished. (She folds her arms).

FATHER. Can we at least agree that the ideal economy should foster substantial economic growth, utilize resources efficiently, distribute the wealth it creates fairly, create economic and social stability, and limit corruption?

(*Amy and Al shake their head in the affirmative. Priscilla shrugs her shoulders, while Charles throws up his hands*).

CHARLES. Business has only one purpose: to make money. Social justice, economic equality, environmental health, and individual morality are not the business of business.

FATHER. Yet business influences, shapes and modifies all these things. Is it any wonder that governments, religions, and citizens' groups want to influence and modify business in return? How well have economic systems other than capitalism addressed these goals Charles?

CHARLES. Socialism might be better at distributing wealth fairly and evenly to its participants, I'll grant you that, but it is a lot less efficient at utilizing resources than capitalism. Under socialism people don't work as hard to earn their living, because they know the government will always take care of them, and managers don't try to cut production or service costs because these don't come directly out of their pocket. (*He looks over at Al*). The government referees may try to make everything run more efficiently in a socialist economy, but what state owned business listens to a referee who can't throw it out of the game? This wastefulness seems to me to be a type of corruption, though I agree that the variety of corruption where large amounts of money change hands in the form of bribes is less likely under socialism than capitalism since it's also less likely that huge amounts of loose money will be floating around in a socialist economy that can be used in this manner.

PRISCILLA. It appears to me that I understand both socialism and capitalism better than either of you. These economic faiths and my spiritual one all know that people are naturally greedy, selfish, self-centered and cruel. Capitalism sees these traits as a positive means to fuel and expand an economy, while socialism recognizes their danger and assigns government the power to reign in some, though not all of them. Socialism allows these traits to continue at the personal level. People can continue to live greedily and selfishly within the superficial limits the government establishes. Socialistic governments allow people to live selfishly as long as their selfish acts are small and evenly distributed among society. It sees this trait as more dangerous only when it is concentrated at the top of the social spectrum since the rich and powerful can impose their selfishness on more people more quickly. When a powerful person takes what others have he can take from thousands all at once, while the people at the bottom usually can steal from only one person at a time. My religion accepts none of this. In my perfect economy of the Kingdom of God people would turn their backs completely on their sinful nature. It will accept no selfishness, no matter how small. Small sins that permeate society cause damage just as large ones do. I think socialism provides a greater threat to the possible redemption of sinners than capitalism. The great sinners of capitalism will refuse to be saved anyway, (*She glances at Charles*). They will always do whatever they please, whereas many of the little sinners (*She looks at Amy*) under socialism could be saved if the government stopped providing an environment that allows them to sin. Charles and I agree on only one thing. The government should step aside and allow the omnipotent power of God to sort it out.

CHARLES. Why thank you Priscilla. Perhaps I've finally found someone else who understands the all-controlling power of natural selection. We're not so different, now are we?

PRISCILLA. (*A look of horror and revulsion spreads across her face*).

CHARLES. With regard to peace and stability, I admit that socialism handles this pretty well, though by no means perfectly. Since there is less competition within a socialist economy there probably will be fewer conflicts between local businesses and more overall business stability; perhaps so much stability that the economy becomes a bit stalled. The participants of a socialist economy will have to compete, however, with the participants of many other economies that operate outside their borders. Many of these economies will consist of the robust, energetic capitalist types. (*He looks around at the rest*). You don't really believe that the whole world will become dominated by socialist economies do you? Since a socialist economy will probably operate less efficiently than these capitalistic competitors they won't be able to thrive unless they raise tariffs or impose other sanctions on its more efficient competitors in order to protect their economy. This might cause other countries to retaliate. Such conflicts rarely become shooting wars, but almost always result in a lowering of the standard of living of the participants of the weaker, less efficient economy.

AL. The socialist Scandinavian countries have a high standard of living. They seem to compete pretty well.

CHARLES. Their standard of living isn't quite as high as ours here under capitalism. Consumer goods cost more, and consumers have less money to spend on them. Businesses may be surviving there but few are triumphing the way our businesses or the businesses of other capitalist oriented countries are. As a result, all of the Scandinavian countries are now taking small steps away from Socialism.

FATHER. There are more economic systems than just capitalism and socialism Charles. What about them?

CHARLES. They are all bit players and major failures compared to capitalism and socialism. Feudalism created little if any wealth. Small amounts of economic growth may have occurred when people opened up new land for agriculture and when they traded for limited amounts of food, raw materials, or hand made products. The only quick path to substantial economic growth occurred when one lord invaded his neighbor to steal his wealth. This produced almost constant warfare Amy. You wouldn't like this economy very much.

AL. Who would?

CHARLES. The nobility controlled nearly all the wealth, of course, but were careful to distribute adequate food and other necessary items to the peasants because they wanted them to be healthy and loyal enough to help defend the nobility's "businesses" against invading neighbors. In some ways you could say that this caused them to distribute the available wealth relatively evenly. Though they held back a much larger share of what little existed for themselves, they hardly possessed a posh lifestyle. Instead the nobility lived cold, short, and uncomfortable lives in close proximity with their serfs. Corruption? Despite the myths about incorruptible knights in shining armor, feudalism didn't really prevent corruption.

FATHER. I'm not sure you could say that feudalism inspired much corruption either since the nobility were openly and unapologetically bent on stealing from each other, and corruption generally tries to hide from sight. Corruption among the peasants was probably also relatively rare, but for a different reason. They lived too much under the close inspection of their lord and neighbors to successfully cheat.

CHARLES. Then there was mercantilism. You would probably like mercantilism

AL. Why? I've never even heard of it.

AMY. What is it?

CHARLES. Under mercantilism government possesses absolute control over the economy, and regulates it solely to make itself stronger, because it considers its interests to be more important than the interests of merchants or anyone else. Although it may allow individuals to invest their own money in businesses and profit from these investments, it does not sustain a truly free market. The government strictly controls these investments, and does everything in its power to ensure that in the end it comes out ahead of everyone else. It may pass laws, tax, and apply tariffs to give these investments an advantage over other countries businesses operating in the world market, but they do so primarily to increase the income of government coffers rather than to increase the investor's profits or raise the over all standard of living for the average person. It sometimes brought great wealth into specific countries, but like capitalism it didn't distribute this wealth evenly among the populace, nor did it distribute it equitably across nations. Usually the successful countries under this system beggared their colonies and lesser rivals. Naturally this system gave rise to long and expensive wars among the countries that were competing economically. If you think capitalism destroys too many lives Amy, you would hate mercantilism. It also allowed much corruption, Priscilla. Here the referees were the star players in the game. Then there was communism. Like your Kingdom of God Priscilla, it existed only in the imaginations of some idealistic fanatics. It never operated in the manner it claimed. People didn't contribute to the economy according to their abilities, nor did they always get what they needed back. Not much wealth was created and economic growth was anemic at best. It utilized human and physical resources incredibly inefficiently, and I can't say that it established much economic stability either when no one knew from day to day if there would be any meat at the local butcher shop. Corruption? You have plenty of corruption when the black market is more reliable than the official one.

AL. If I hear you correctly, none of the existing economic systems meet all the criteria of the perfect economy.

FATHER. (*Smiles and nods in Al's direction*). There are no perfect economic systems. Economics has been called the dismal science because it really doesn't offer any permanent answers. Sooner or later all economic programs will collapse (*Priscilla smiles with satisfaction*) under their own weight. Feudalism, mercantilism, socialism, communism, all fail to deliver eternal, continuous economic growth and constant improvement a society's standard of living. Charles, you claim to understand economics. Why is that the case?

CHARLES. A permanent though largely invisible substructure supports all economic systems. Politicians like Al may try to circumvent these immutable laws, but it is impossible to do so. The problem with every economic system devised by humanity is that we deny these laws rather than accept them… though I believe that capitalism accepts more of these laws than the other economic systems do.

FATHER. There may be more at play here than economic laws, but I am pleased that you admit that none of the economic systems already created by mankind have always provided the economic well being, stability and fairness we desire. I'm puzzled, however, why you think that some barely visible economic natural laws offer a more solid sort of certainty instead. Don't you see a problem with your logic?

CHARLES. (*Shakes his head "no"*).

FATHER. What kind of basic economic laws are you talking about then?

CHARLES. The law of supply and demand would be one of these laws.

PRISCILLA. Ah yes, I've heard it called the invisible hand of God.

CHARLES. Whatever

FATHER. The operation of any "God's" hand in every economic transaction does seem to be invisible, if it really exists at all. How can you be so certain that the law of supply and demand is an absolutely universal and permanently "natural law"?

CHARLES. There is no uncertainty here for you to chew on Father. Economics rests on the well-documented investigation of human nature. The law of supply and demand has been objectively tested many times in the marketplace, with real people and real money.

FATHER. Yes, yes, human nature, and the marketplace. Nothing uncertain about either of those. What other certainties about economics do you want us to believe?

CHARLES. All economic activity is a zero sum game. When one participant gains another loses. Economic survival is always a struggle. Darwin's Law of the Fittest determines economic survival in the same way that it determines survival in the natural world. There will always be economic winners and losers and there is nothing that Al and his kind can do about it. He should just sit back and let the winners dispatch the losers as painlessly as possible.

FATHER. Your libertarian slant on capitalism, Charles, focuses only on one of its aspects. While I agree that capitalism relies on competition for its dynamism and ability to create new products and economic growth, you are wrong to claim that it is essentially a zero sum game. Capitalism could foster economic benefits for everyone, both your so-called winners and losers. When an economy grows, the economy's overall wealth also increases, and that wealth can be distributed to all of the economy's participants if capitalists and the government allow it. Everyone becomes a winner. There are few losers in a growing economy if it shares the wealth that it has created equitably. Capitalism can be a win-win environment rather that an all or nothing situation.

PRISCILLA. You're living in as much of a dream world as Amy does. Human history has shown that economic growth can only exist temporarily. It doesn't matter what economic system you happen to implement. Eventually, every man made system will fail. You've already seen the destruction that capitalism brought down upon us during the last economic downturn. How much pain are you willing to suffer before you abandon your belief that capitalism or any economic system will always carry everyone onward and upward? Only faith in God can do that.

AL. After each downturn, economic growth returned and made us all wealthier. The most lethal and destructive wars and pandemics eventually ushered in the most robust and long lasting economic and cultural recoveries. It's always darkest before the dawn.

AMY. (*Brightens up and smiles.*)

PRISCILLA. A recovery has occurred recently, but it can't go on forever. Ultimately there'll be another great economic downturn, which, as Charles acknowledges, no economic system can prevent. This might even lead to final apocalypse that the Bible accurately predicts, no matter whose economic system is in place.

CHARLES. Hmm. Interesting, you see an economic collapse in much the same way as I see a species collapse in the natural world. I'm starting to understand your otherwise deluded vision Priscilla.

AL. Why does an economic collapse have to be so inevitable? We humans are much more intelligent, resourceful, and flexible than any of the other species inhabiting this planet's natural world.

FATHER. You've made a good point. Yes every economic system, every economic solution eventually threatens to undermine and destroy itself, but we humans are resourceful enough to work around this so that it does not become a foregone conclusion.

AMY. I don't understand. How do solutions destroy themselves?

CHARLES. All economies operate within the natural world and follow many of the same patterns that regulate this world. One repeated pattern found both in economics and nature is that when a species or an economic system becomes too successful in its location it begins to change this location in ways that ultimately limits its success.

AL. What are you talking about? Everyone knows nothing succeeds like success.

CHARLES. For example, you might come upon a fertile piece of ground and begin planting corn on it. For the first few years it will produce bumper crops, but as you use it year after year you will start to notice a decline in production. If you continue to use this same wealth creator you will eventually experience a total crop failure.

FATHER. (*Nodding in agreement.*) Likewise, if investors pile into the same investment year after year its price may exceed what it ever could be worth. This will become apparent to investors, and they will drive the price down to more reasonable levels. Growth industries will also lose their potential for growth as more an more competitors enter that industry. Not only individual investments but also whole systems of economic thought can follow this same pattern. Capitalism will work fine, until we overuse it. Then we will need to adjust it somehow in order for it to continue to work. That's where our human resourcefulness comes in to play. In the cornfield we can add fertilizer, plant cover crops, or simply give the field a rest for a few years before returning it to production. We humans have the ability to similarly fix an economic problem or even an economic system despite the probable inevitability that no economic solution will work forever. We possess the intellectual and emotional potential to clean up our failures and/or move on. We don't have to passively accept the boom and bust of our current economy or any of its other drawbacks.

CHARLES. I appreciate that you recognize the authority of this particular law of nature, but your optimism ignores one of the other important ones. We live in a finite world that contains finite resources. Eventually we will run out of something necessary to keep our economies growing. The population will rise to the point where there is no possible way everyone can have a job. Inflation will impoverish everyone who has husbanded his or her financial resources and depression will impoverish everyone who has not. People will scramble for whatever bits of wealth remain. Some people will die. Everyone will suffer. Civilization will dim. You can't think a way out of this certain impasse.

PRISCILLA. And there is nothing anyone can do except wait for the coming of the Kingdom of God.

AMY. You sound like you're looking forward to an apocalyptic collapse Priscilla.

PRISCILLA. I am. I want to see justice finally be done. I want to see all the sinners that have stained this world dragged to their deserved perdition.

AMY. Such a collapse will cause everyone, even those you consider to be innocent to suffer.

PRISCILLA. No God will save them by ushering them into the Kingdom of God.

AMY. They will certainly suffer horribly before He does, and I don't even see why God should torment someone like Charles, who heartless as he may be, honestly believes that what he has done and plans to do is reasonable and correct. How can you call yourself a Christian? Where is your Christian charity for saint and sinner alike?

PRISCILLA. My Christian charity was stolen by the greedy and corrupt (*She glances over at Charles and Al*). I've had to close my food bank because people selfishly think only of themselves and have stopped donating to it, and in Africa, local government troops are trying to close the mission I was supporting. This world is a filthy place Amy, (*She stares angrily at Amy*), that I cannot scrub clean. It's better that it's all destroyed.

AL. A revolutionary sentiment if I've ever heard one. I'm starting to think that Charles is right about you.

FATHER. And you Charles, you're sounding less and less like a capitalist, even a libertarian capitalist, and more and more like a eighteenth century Malthusian. Your pessimism about the future is almost as complete as Priscilla's, though at least you don't predict the end of the world.

AMY. What is a Malthusian? Is it some sort of scientific system that Charles believes in?

FATHER. A Malthusian is someone who believes in the discredited ideas of the economist Thomas Robert Malthus who predicted that the world's population would grow faster than it could grow its food supplies and that civilization could soon crash through mass starvation, or that pockets of starvation would keep the world's population from growing beyond a certain level. He underestimated humanity's ability to improve existing methods of growing food or to create new ones. We also developed ways to reduce food waste and global food imbalances by inventing refrigeration and making the transport of food more efficient and fast. Today the world's population has grown many times larger than it was in Malthus' time and continues to grow. Pockets of starvation do occur, but usually because of political conflicts rather than to actual lack of food.

CHARLES. Yes Malthus' predictions have proven to be wrong so far. I don't think that society will crumble due to starvation, but we needn't discard all of his ideas. The rapid increase of the world's population is indeed creating serious economic problems. We may not be facing immediate mass starvation, but a major economic disaster still may be in store for all of us because world population is growing faster than the resources needed to sustain it.

AL. Nothing government can't handle, I'm sure.

FATHER. Some governments have responded to the stresses of population growth better than others.

CHARLES. I have a theory that population growth might be the key factor behind all of our economic problems.

AL. Really? Let's hear your theory.

CHARLES. I think that the best measure of a country's economic health is to divide the "economic mass" of that country's economy by the number of people living in that country. The larger the number, the healthier the economy.

AL. What is this "economic mass"?

CHARLES. It is not just cash, nor wealth in the form of other liquid assets, nor how fast money is traveling from person to person within the economy. It includes all three factors.

AL. Why not just call it wealth? If you did, I'd understand what you're talking about. The more people there are the smaller each person's fair share of the existing wealth would be. You know, like wealth is a pie and the more slices you have to cut the smaller each piece becomes. That I can understand. I constantly have to make decisions about the size of everybody's pie.

CHARLES. The idea of wealth doesn't include the third factor in "economic mass", how quickly money moves around in an economy.

AMY. I know money passes through my hands pretty quickly. Does that mean I have "economic mass"?

CHARLES. In a limited way, yes. An economy exists only at the moment when an economic transaction occurs. If no buying and selling occurs, a country's "economic mass" is tiny no matter how much wealth its participants are holding. For example, sometimes the Romans bribed many barbarian tribes with pieces of silver to remain peaceful. Quite often barbarian chieftains would horde this silver by burying it, perhaps for future use, rather than spend it and send it circulating throughout the barbarian economy. Archeologists still occasionally find these hordes. You could consider this unused silver a form of wealth, but since it was never used, and perhaps never intended to be used, we shouldn't consider it as part of the barbarian economy's "economic mass". "Economic mass" only materializes when someone uses his wealth in the form of currency or other liquid assets to acquire something else. The more often and faster people purchase something, the more vibrant and healthy the economy within which these people operate becomes. A person buys a coat from a tailor and pays cash. The tailor takes that cash to buy a chair from a carpenter, and the carpenter uses it to buy groceries for his family. The amount of money in circulation has not grown since the Federal Reserve Bank first created it, but each transaction increases the size and strength of the economy. The "economic mass" of an economy possesses some of the characteristics of a motion picture. A slow projector displays a halting jerkiness of annoying gaps, but when the projector speeds up it displays an image that is robust, comprehensible, and lifelike. It begins to appear real and substantial The same thing occurs to an economy when its number of transaction increase and speed up. Al, you remove money from the economy that could otherwise propel the number and speed of that economy's transactions when you raise taxes. These taxes will reduce that economy's "economic mass" and make the economy weaker and less dynamic.

PRISCILLA. This would also happen whenever money becomes concentrated into a few hands that are reluctant to spend. Reducing their taxes won't necessarily strengthen the economy either if they don't spread that money around. If people were more charitable, this would more likely strengthen the economy than a tax reduction. Am I right?

CHARLES. (*Waves her away dismissively and continues*). In these cases, the numerator in my formula decreases, the economy starts to wither, and a recession or even a depression may result. Likewise, even if an economy's "economic mass remains the same, an increase in the population size located in the denominator will produce the same result. This is why the world economy has been struggling like it has. Its population is growing faster than the world economy's economic mass".

FATHER. What evidence do you have that such a relationship between your 'economic mass' and increased population exists?

CHARLES. The European economy exploded during the Renaissance after large portions of the population died in the great plagues of the Middle Ages. Similar economic growth occurred after the first and second world wars. Recently we've seen world poverty grow and economies slow as populations have increased worldwide. He rate of economic growth is currently smaller than that of population growth. This results in the amount of buying power for each individual to decline. Poverty results. Standards of living decline. People are unhappy, (*looks over at Al and smiles.*), and people get voted out of office.

PRISCILLA. No, more people are poor today because greedy people like you have grasped a hold of more than their fair of the world's wealth. (*Amy nods in agreement*).

CHARLES. (*Shrugs*). I'm sure that an unequal distribution of the existing "economic mass" hasn't improved the situation any, but the larger, more intractable problem for governments is their population growth exceeding the growth of its economic mass which results in a reduction of their citizen's buying power, and, in turn, standard of living.

FATHER. You're the one who always worships facts. What facts do you have to support this theory?

CHARLES. The world's population is clearly growing faster than ever. That is a fact.

FATHER. Wouldn't an increase in population also increase the number of economic transactions and the velocity at which money circulates? That should increase the world economy's "economic mass". The additional people the world carries need to buy food, clothing, and other necessities.

CHARLES. Most of the population increase involves people who do not possess enough money to make the purchases they normally would if they were wealthier. While population growth may increase the number of economic transactions somewhat, the rate of buying and selling of these additional people lowers the average rate of transactions per person for the world economy as a whole.

FATHER. What factual evidence do you have about the growth rate of the world's "economic mass?"

CHARLES. Well…it's difficult to establish… what that is, I agree, but we can look at gross national products, manufacturing data, and national money supplies and make an educated guess.

AL. You're guessing? (*He throws his hands up in desperation*).

FATHER. You claim you factor in other assets besides actual currency in your calculation of "economic mass". How do you determine what these are worth?

CHARLES. The value of other assets such as stocks and bonds can be easily ascertained by referring to their current market value.

AL. That change from minute to minute.

FATHER. Yes, and the value of less liquid assets such as real estate, gold coins, and fine art are even more difficult to nail down. These assets may possess an appraised value, but their true value can't be calculated until they are sold. How can you factor these into your calculation of "economic mass"?

CHARLES. Like I said, it's an estimate. Probably these less liquid assets shouldn't be included in the calculation.

FATHER. In fact you can't calculate "economic mass" even at its most basic level until you actually engage in an economic transaction. A buyer knows he has the ability to purchase a bushel of wheat only when a seller has agreed to sell it for a price the buyer can afford. One day the buyer may have enough wealth to purchase a certain amount of wheat and the next day he may not. On the day he does not, your "economic mass" must wither a bit because no transaction took place. This "economic mass" idea is vague and fluid, and its actual rate of increase or decrease is a mystery. How can you create a formula where the numerator will always be uncertain? Are you sure you want to promote this theory?

CHARLES. It's only a theory, a place to start thinking.

FATHER. Indeed it is only that. Even undisputed numbers like the amounts on deposit in a nation's banks cause problems in your calculation of "economic mass". If a country begins to print more money to stimulate the economy, the value of that money might decline and its value decline with it. How do you factor that into your calculations?

CHARLES. All right, I don't. I admit a firm calculation of "economic mass" is not yet available. The only point I want to make here is that the only way to reduce poverty and increase a society's economic well being is to increase economic activity by growing the economy, and it might help if population growth slowed down a little so that the fruits of this economic growth wouldn't be watered down so quickly. Right now it doesn't look like this is ever going to happen, especially if we have to rely on politicians like

AL. Ah yes, again, it's my fault. While Charles doesn't believe I can develop any useful solutions to our economic problems, I'll bet he'd like me to find one so he can criticize as inadequate anything I propose. Priscilla, on the other hand, doesn't seem to care if I ever find a solution. She has little interest in the problems with which I have to deal except to the extent that they affect human character or her sense of injured justice. She believes humanity's eventual comfort and joy lies beyond economics. Neither one of them has provided me with anything useful. Amy? Well she IS full of ideas, but they are so impractical that no one else here believes I could possibly implement them. This meeting you put together Pops is a royal waste of time. I'm no closer to fixing the economy than I was when I walked in the door.

FATHER. You surprise me. I've never seen you give up so easily in the face of a stiff challenge. Your brother and sisters may have offered less than helpful opinions, but there may be something useful hidden in what they have to offer. (*Charles looks up in shocked surprise, Priscilla continues to scowl, and Amy smiles vaguely*). You've always been able to make something useful out of scraps of ideas thrown out by others. Do you remember the summer when you were ten and we spent three weeks at the camp up at the lake? You wanted to make a little birdhouse for some bluebirds you saw in the trees. We had no carpentry tools at the camp, and very little lumber, so you crafted your bird house with a butcher knife, a small hammer used to crack ice you found next to the sink in the bar, twine and small branches from the pine tree next to our cabin.

AL. (*Begins to smile and nods his head affirmatively*).

PRISCILLA. That birdhouse was as ugly.

CHARLES. I distinctly remember telling you that the opening was too large for bluebirds, and I was correct, as usual.

AMY. (*Laughs*). It *was* pretty ugly, but a pair of Robins used it as a nesting spot the following year. I remember how we all enjoyed watching them raise their chicks.

AL. It **WAS** a success wasn't it? (*He looks at his father and smiles knowingly*). I'll bet I can build something you will all find rewarding with nothing more than the string, sticks, and the tools the three of you have provided

CHARLES. You don't know enough about economics to build anything.

AL. Don't be so sure about that. I'll bet I have a lot more experience dealing with people who handle money than you do. (*He smiles to himself*).

PRISCILLA. You know nothing about the spiritual implications of money, how it corrupts our understanding of God's creation, or how it destroys what God deems the proper relationship people should maintain between each other.

AL. That is to say that I don't begin my search for economic solutions with the many prejudices about money and its uses that adhere to you.

FATHER. That's good to hear. How do you plan to proceed from here?

THE DEVIL IS IN THE DETAILS?

AL. My first step will be to better understand what tools I have at hand, (*He glances at his brother and sisters*), and how I can best use them to craft a solution.

PRISCILLA. I'm not your tool! I'm a Christian with an immortal soul that is not at your disposal but at God's. I possess free will and freely choose the values that God wants me to choose. I freely reject whatever scheme you're planning.

AMY. I don't reject what you are planning because I don't know what it is. I'm pretty sure I can help you a lot more then these two, (*she gestures toward Priscilla and Charles*), who have their heads stuck somewhere up in the clouds. I know more about the economy than they do because I'm mired in the middle of it. I can tell you exactly what it looks like, smells like, and tastes like.

CHARLES. (*Smirks*) That's why you can't clearly see any reasonable solutions. You are too much a part of the problem. I, on the other hand, can coolly and calmly step back from the problem to analyze any ideas that Al might develop. I can be objective while you are trapped by the subjectivity of your senses. When you possess my type of detachment, affection and judgment need not make war with each other. *(Adam Phillips) I'm the only one here who knows that an immutable mathematical reality exists independently of the human mind and its foolish human emotions. This reality holds more permanence than the physical reality that you all perceive around you. *(Alain Cannes) If you are seeking a permanent solution to our economic problems Al, you must find it within the eternal mathematical truths. I'm the only one here who possesses the tools to understand these truths.

AL. Your mathematical reality sounds a bit like Priscilla's Kingdom of God, all clean and shiny and perfect.

CHARLES. (*Sputters indignantly*). It is nothing at all like Priscilla's benighted superstitions. She sets out searching for her twisted version of "truth" with a collection of judgments and beliefs already frozen in place. She then builds other judgments upon these false ones until she arrives at conclusions she always expected to reach.

FATHER. You start out with the false belief that you don't carry any pre-existing beliefs and that you can really understand all of the world's complications objectively. You believe that reason can establish a foolproof foundation for understanding the world.

CHARLES. (*A little rattled.*) Well, you have to start somewhere.

FATHER. Yes, you do. You have to accept whatever beliefs you happen to hold at the beginning of your search for truth, but you should question all them all and put them aside when they block rather than aid your progress.

AL. Pops will these mathematical truths that Charles prefers actually help me solve the messy problems I face?

FATHER. You might want to at least listen to him. As Aristotle pointed out, there may be no perfect mathematical entities in this world, but there are plainly imperfect approximations. He might give you some ideas for imperfect though useable solutions.

AL. O.K. Charles let's start out with one of your so-called laws that you mentioned earlier. How does the law of supply and demand operate?

CHARLES. (*Clears his throat*). Whenever a lot of an item exists, people will prize it less highly, that is to say the demand for it declines, and as a result, its price declines. When something becomes scarce, the demand for it increases and it becomes more expensive.

AL. I've heard this law repeated many times by my advisors. It makes sense. I understand that capital markets reflect this law all of the time. When money is scarce, you have to pay more interest to borrow some. Money becomes more valuable when there is less of it in circulation. Some of my advisors recommended that we solve our economic problems by increasing the amount of money in circulation and by lowering interest rates. When the Federal Reserve did this, my advisors were very happy. I guess it helped the economy by encouraging people to borrow and spend more, but I'm really not certain it was the best remedy because other advisors have indicated that it was a serious mistake and will only establish greater problems in the future. Who should I believe?

CHARLES. I never said the law of supply and demand was a foolproof answer to fixing an economy. I'm saying it operates as one unvarying characteristic of every economy.

FATHER. I'm not so sure you can even say that. Does the law of supply and demand really operate like a physical law, such as the law of gravity, everywhere, every time and in the same manner?

CHARLES. Absolutely. By definition, the law of supply and demand will apply everywhere, at all times, and in the same manner.

FATHER. Then I don't believe that the law of supply and demand constitutes a natural law.

CHARLES. Well, it is. (*He folds his arms.*)

FATHER. If someone holds all of some needed item, such as gasoline, both the supply and demand can be large at the same time. Your law simply doesn't apply in this case. What will limit the demand for the gasoline here isn't the amount available for sale, but the price the supplier wants to receive for it. The supplier could be holding a huge volume of gasoline and be willing to sell it all but at a price he, rather than the market, would determine. As a result, the demand for his gasoline it wouldn't decrease even though a glut of it might exist. People would still need and want the gasoline, but many customers couldn't afford it at the supplier's price. The supplier might continue to raise his price until it reached a point where no one could afford to buy any at all. The price might then fall, but not because either the supply or the demand for gasoline has fallen, but because the amount of money that people could allocate to this purchase was limited.

CHARLES. Monopolies like the one you describe are rare.

PRISCILLA. You'd try to establish one if you could.

AL. Don't worry; governments generally protect people from such monopolies Priscilla.

CHARLES. (*Ignoring them both*). Anyway father, I could argue that raising prices above what most people can afford is in itself a kind of reduction of the supply. Finally, competition will always exist in one form or another. If someone establishes a monopoly someone else will try to take advantage of the high prices by breaking into the business and underselling the monopolist, or, as Al indicates, the government will find a way to interfere and introduce a government sponsored competitor into the situation. Competition from other commercial suppliers generally offers the best method to take down a monopoly. The ubiquity and power of private sector competition forms another economic natural law.

AL. Let me remind you that the government and not private sector competitors broke up John D Rockefeller's oil monopoly. Some monopolies may become so large and powerful that only the government can dissolve them. Forgetting about monopolies for the moment, why didn't the law of supply and demand apply to those financial derivatives that the banks and I lost so much money over during the most recent financial meltdown?

CHARLES. What are you talking about? I'm sure that the law of supply and demand applied to them just like it does to everything else.

AL. The supply of these derivatives did not change significantly between the day before their values crashed and the day after, yet the demand for them plummeted, and many became worthless. Demand changed dramatically although supply barely moved.

CHARLES. You're wrong. While the number that existed didn't change, the number that went up for sale ballooned did when they were dumped onto the market all at once. That increased the supply for sale and that, in turn, cratered their price. The supply of goods and services that matter are the ones that people are trying actively to sell and not what happens to exist.

AL. But why did the demand drop so swiftly? Why did the supply mushroom so unexpectedly for no apparent reason? What economic natural law caused that?

CHARLES. Some vagary of human nature I'm sure. (He waves his hand dismissively). What is certain is that the relationship between supply and demand functioned as it should and as it always will during panic selling. This relationship has been proven mathematically many times. There's no point arguing against the existence of this relationship.

AL. A lot of good this law will do me if it can't predict and help me evade economic calamities. You can prove many things with statistics that aren't very useful.

CHARLES. Well, oh pragmatic one, every day people like you consider the relationship between supply and demand when they set and accept the prices of goods and services. It's a common and very real activity. If you want the law of supply and demand to teach you a lesson, I would say it is "Don't panic".

AL. (*Nods his head in understanding*). That's good advice, but doesn't happen to be very mathematical at all.

FATHER. I don't see how your law of supply and demand will guarantee that people will always come up with the fairest and most effective prices for an economy as a whole.

CHARLES. It always works. Individuals may make mistakes in valuing goods and services, but markets as a whole come to the correct price through the influence of this law.

AL. Were the markets correct the day before the meltdown or the day after?

CHARLES. They were correct both days.

AL. (*Rolls his eyes*). Then why did owning them feel like such a mistake in determining their true value?

FATHER. I don't believe that economists can prove a constant relationship between supply and demand because in the supplier/buyer relationship they can measure only the supplier's point of view accurately. They can count the supply of something but not measure accurately buyer's desires.

AL. Don't economists measure both?

FATHER. You can easily measure the supply of a good or service if everyone tells the truth about their inventories, production, and staffing. Which I don't think economists can guarantee either, but demand is based on human emotions. Desires and personal needs vary from person to person and constantly change within each individual. The level of a person's desire for some item or service would be difficult to measure even if it weren't constantly in motion. We can measure demand accurately only after the fact, that is, after the transaction has occurred, and even this measurement doesn't take into consideration the demand that was not fulfilled by the purchase. Pent up demand for goods and services cannot be accurately measured any more accurately than any other action prior to its occurrence.

CHARLES. It can be by aggregating surveys and sales data and projecting future demand from this solid information. Also, the aggregate price of an item as it is sold across an economy provides an accurate picture of the demand for that item.

FATHER. A straight-line projection of past sales I suppose? What in this life ever moves constantly in a straight line?

CHARLES. Sure, projections can be incorrect, but you can easily determine the demand for an item at the moment.

FATHER. How?

CHARLES. Through the current price of the item as it is sold.

FATHER. The day a new I-Phone goes on sale the demand for it is so great that a long line will extend out the front door of each Apple store. Two days later there is no line. To me, this indicates that the demand for an I-Phone has lessoned somewhat. The price stays the same, however. Isn't the line a better indication of current demand than the price? The price was determined not by accurately measuring demand, but by evaluating production costs, adding on desired profit margins, and speculating what future demand will be.

CHARLES. Over time the I Pod's price will drop as more and more people buy one and satisfy their desire to own one. This drop in price parallels the drop in the public's demand to own one.

FATHER. How does price measure the demand for an I-Pod for those who can't afford to buy one? Shouldn't they be included in any measurement of the overall demand for the item?

CHARLES. When the price drops to a level these people can afford, they will purchase it and support that price by reducing the supply at that price level.

FATHER. What happens to that demand if the price never drops to a level these people can afford?

CHARLES. If the price never drops to a level a person can afford, he or she never becomes part of the supply-demand equation. In other words his demand for the item falls outside the law. It's beside the point.

FATHER. I don't know how you can be so sure about that. Isn't it possible that any person's desire for the item helps support the desire of others who can afford to buy it? Haven't you just given us another exception to your immutable law?

AMY. I would really like a diamond necklace Charles, as they find more diamonds will that increase the supply to the point where I can afford to buy one?

AL. Probably not, since DeBeers works diligently to limit the amount of diamonds on the market so that prices remain high.

CHARLES. So what point are you trying to make father?

FATHER. This so called 'natural law' of yours, or if you prefer Priscilla, this "invisible hand of God" can sometimes be a useful tool, but is not worthy of any blind faith. You believe in an economic 'natural law' that is based at least partly on the vagaries of human emotion, and that can't be measured with the absolute certainty you assume.

CHARLES. Whether certain or not, my insights are more valuable than your constant doubts about the laws of economics and human nature.

FATHER. (*Shakes his head vigorously in the negative*). The reality behind my cosmic doubts will probably have a greater effect on any solutions that Al constructs than the mathematical reality in which you seem to live. Al, I'd advise you to look beyond economic laws for any solution to the serious problems your constituents are experiencing. Don't ignore them, of course. Perceiving a vague pattern where Charles sees a law governing these elements can be very useful. I suggest only that you reserve a little bit of doubt about the ultimate truth of this pattern when you make your plans.

AL. In other words, you want me to understand the uncertainty supporting this "natural law" as much as I understand its validity. You want me to treat this "truth" like I do all the other "truths" people try to foist upon me. (*He glances over to Priscilla*).

FATHER. (*Nods affirmatively*). I know I don't have to preach to you about the power of uncertainty.

AL. Heh, I know it well.

CHARLES. Al, you would be making a mistake to doubt the law of supply and demand or any other proven economic law, just as you did when you doubted the profitability of my research project. I made a great deal of money from that project, while you sold out your shares at the first sign of trouble. You need to believe, not doubt reasonable conclusions and rational processes.

AL. I believe them only when I see them work. You made your money by selling your process to a greater fool than you. I've heard your "rational" buyer has filed for bankruptcy. I won't be placing all my faith in your reasonable "facts" any time soon.

CHARLES. It seems to me that my reason saved me a lot of money when I sold out. Remember that when you develop your economic plans

PRISCILLA. Your reason in this case sounds more like a source of deception rather than a source of truth.

THE JUNGLE

CHARLES. (*He looks at Al*). There is another economic law though, that you, Al, cannot disagree with.

AL. What's that?.

CHARLES. Competition for limited resources and success will always dominate any desired economic system that we expect to endure.

AL. I've certainly spent my entire life competing for one thing or another, and I've always embraced competition as a wonderful experience. So yes, I agree with you absolutely.

AMY. (*Looks confused*). It doesn't sound so good to me.

AL. Competition is especially dominant in a Capitalist system. It's what makes so effective and useful. It forces us to try harder, and because we try, we produce more and better quality goods and services. Competition in a Capitalist system creates progress and this progress results in wealth and a better general standard of living. I disagree with those who claim that all economic systems end up as zero sum games with winners taking their gains only from the losers. (*He looks at Charles*). They make competition sound depressing and hopeless, and like something we should but can't avoid.

CHARLES. You should neither embrace nor avoid it. Just accept it. You have no choice in the matter. Competition pre-existed human civilization and has woven itself inextricably into reality. It is more powerful than civilization, than any religion, human affection, and even more powerful than all human thought. In fact, competition is the driving force that lies behind all of these human creations and all living existence.

AMY. Your belief in the inevitability of competition, Charles, sounds just as heartless as Priscilla's unforgiving religion. (*She glances briefly at Priscilla.*)

CHARLES. (*He ignores Amy.*) Competition determines what is most fit to survive in the natural world, and economic activity certainly resides in this natural world. You must agree don't you, Father?

FATHER. While I don't agree that competition ensures that the best always survives, I do see some benefit in considering an economy as a living creature whose problems mimic some of the same ones that living creatures experience.

AMY. (*Brightens up*). You mean that sometimes the economy acts like a puppy?

FATHER. (*Smiles*), Yes to the extent that both economies and puppies get sick from time to time and need some type of care to become well again.

CHARLES. Um, yes, like less regulation and lower taxes.

AL. Or, maybe lower interest rates?

PRISCILLA. Maybe we can heal our sick economy by putting all the greedy bankers in jail or in some other way limiting 's corruption.

AMY. Maybe giving us all a little more money to spend.

FATHER. Except for jailing bankers, these remedies have all been applied in the past. They often worked to one degree or another in much the same way that antibiotics have been used to cure biological diseases. In both contexts the solutions don't seem to be working as well as they did in the past. Physical ailments and economic ones can both develop a resistance to their treatments, and where such a resistance hasn't developed, we often find that the remedies act like chemotherapy with the medicine destroying not only the disease but also healthy parts of the body and the economy. Like we do with medicine you need to develop new remedies, or combine old ones, if you are to heal the economy, I'd recommend that you not simply fall back on a traditional remedy, to fix our ailing economy. You need to be constantly developing new solutions if you are going to stay ahead of its constantly changing problems.

CHARLES. Nonsense. You don't need to think up anything new at all. Sit back and let nature take care of everything. Allow the omnipotent law of the survival of the fittest to sort out the economy. It will strengthen and thrive as a result.

FATHER. How do you define "the fittest"?

CHARLES. Those that succeed and survive are the fittest. After the less fit economies inevitably perish, the more fit capitalist ones will grow like never before.

FATHER. That's a matter of blind faith, and not of fact.

CHARLES. No, the law of the survival of the fittest has been validated over and over again, both in the laboratory and on the street. It is a law that would operate even if people did not exist to understand it or believe in it.

FATHER. That statement itself constitutes an act of faith, much like Priscilla's belief in the omnipotence of her god. I can't imagine any fact or principle that I would always accept under any circumstance. Fallible humans have created all of them, and when we apply them onto other people, we apply them onto people equally fallible and unpredictable.

CHARLES. The law of the survival of the fittest existed long before people did. People didn't create it; they found it, and this natural law underlies all economic activity.

FATHER. Surely we have the duty to question such an important economic law if we are to fully understand how economies really operate. Who dictated what was fittest before people were around to do so?

CHARLES. Nature defined what was most fit by allowing only the fittest to survive. You are the fittest when you survive and others don't.

FATHER. Your law doesn't predict anything. It's based on circular logic. If you survive, your fit, and if you're fit you survive. Your law has no legitimate use that I can see. Though I see plenty of illegitimate uses.

PRISCILLA. God sent his son so that we could be saved from death and enter into an eternal life that transcends death. The fittest, in God's eyes are those who put their trust in this fact, and not those who are the last to die.

AL. (*Ignoring Priscilla.*) Charles, you oppose even modest levels of government regulation and intervention based on an argument that Pops says leads us nowhere?

CHARLES. Any attempts by the government to "fix" our economy will be futile, and a waste of time and resources. I understand Darwin's laws better than any of you, and know that you are doomed to fail whenever you try to oppose the inevitability of this law.

FATHER. Charles, your knowledge of Darwin's work is not as factual as you think. Darwin never coined the term "survival of the fittest" in any of his writings. Herbert Spencer, a political and social conservative whose ideas have been widely discredited made up the term long after Darwin had published his Origin of Species. Spenser, unlike Darwin was "unequivocally and fanatically opposed to all government programs that he viewed as obstacles to social selection including public education, and health regulations."* (Susan Jacoby) I believe he even opposed a government-sponsored postal service. The American William Graham Sumner, applied the term later still to sociology and economics. Sumner is famous for writing "A drunkard in the gutter is just where he ought to be, according to the fitness and tendency of things. Nature has set upon him the process of decline and dissolution by which she removes things which have survived their usefulness." On the other hand, Darwin believed that empathy and compassion might promote evolutionary benefits. I could argue that based on this theory of Darwin's the most fit societies and economic systems would be those whose members took care of each other.

CHARLES. (*Looks blankly at his father*). Well, maybe Spenser was right. The Post Office operates at a loss. Packages are lost. There must be a more efficient system that should replace it. Anyway, Spencer's and Sumner's ideas were certainly based on Darwin's. You can't deny that. (*He turns quickly to Al*). You should have the courage of your capitalist convictions instead of flip flopping all over the place like a dying fish whenever father comes up with some new question or doubt. You once told me that you didn't believe in most of the government regulations you put in place.

AL. (*Smiles weakly*). I never disbelieved in them either.

CHARLES. We don't need government regulation because nature regulates everything. The economy is already regulated by the natural laws of existence. I've already shown how one of those laws, the law of supply and demand coordinates markets, but there are others too. The "survival of the fittest" is another of these laws.

FATHER. How does this law of the fittest "regulate" markets and the economy as a whole?

CHARLES. They weed out weak and inefficient businesses and economic practices and replace them with better, cheaper, more useful alternatives. The same laws of evolution lie behind economic and social progress. Al, you should be encouraging the fittest economy possible, because you should want an economy that promotes progress and survives as long as possible.

AL. O.K. That's a legitimate goal.

CHARLES. In order for this to happen you must induce a creative destruction that replaces outmoded practices with more successful ones. The natural law of evolution does this much better than government ever can. You government officials feel sorry for the inefficient ones who must be swept away to make way for the new. The laws of evolution blindly and without prejudice weed out inefficient businesses to continually produce a stronger and better economy.

AMY. But it hasn't produced a stronger and better economy. Right now the economy's a mess. Clearly your economic laws of evolution don't work.

AL. Amy's right. The "creative destruction" you favor has given us more destruction and very little creation.

CHARLES. You just need to wait a little while longer to see the results. Evolution never makes changes overnight. It takes a while for "creative destruction" to work. That's why it's called evolution and not revolution. In time the market's methods of self-regulation will work out for the best. That is, it will eventually work out if the government doesn't stick its greasy fingers into the mix.

FATHER. This sounds a bit like Priscilla's "kingdom of god" where everything works out in the end if you only keep the faith and hold on. Wouldn't it be better for us humans to regulate and create solutions for our economic problems as they occur rather than to wait for god or nature to take care of it? We could reduce an awful lot of human suffering if we stepped up to solve our own problems.

CHARLES. Human efforts could also make the suffering worse by making it last longer.

PRISCILLA. Suffering is a necessary part of the human condition and necessary for our ultimate redemption.

CHARLES. (*nods*). I would modify that thought somewhat, Priscilla, by saying that suffering is a necessary part of economic healing and progress.

PRISCILLA. Suffering ennobles us and makes us worthy of God's love.

CHARLES. (*Charles makes a face*). It's an inevitable part of existence. (*Priscilla shakes her head and turns away from Charles*).

AMY. Suffering hurts. No sane person can like it and wish for more. (*She stares at Charles and Priscilla uncomprehendingly*).

AL. (*Glumly*). I can't run on a platform that suffering is good for my constituents in the long run.

AMY. If you want my vote Al, you have to show me how you will help people suffer less and enjoy life more rather than lecture me about how beautiful the light at the end of some spiritual or scientific tunnel might someday become.

CHARLES. His efforts would be a waste of time. The government's puny attempts to make people happy are no match for the forces of natural selection and the law of the fittest. All your efforts at regulation and establishing government funded social programs will fail in the long run when pitted against nature's implacable will. Only the strong, crafty and unfettered will survive no matter what government tries to do. Sooner or later everyone will realize that their interest in surviving will prevent them from treating each other kindly. There will not be enough wealth and resources to sustain everyone and an economic collapse will result no matter what government programs or schemes are in place. When this happens, the only people who will survive will be those who don't share and instead keep all available resources for themselves. You wouldn't survive a weekend under those conditions, Amy.

AMY. Good. I wouldn't want to survive in such a horrid world! (*Priscilla smiles*).

FATHER. You seem to think that the law of the jungle will always triumph over the laws of civilization. This is untrue. Natural laws may determine some aspects of our economy's structure and direction, but human beings create the lion's share of this out of their own intellect.

CHARLES. Government cannot undo the natural struggle that forms the very fabric of existence.

PRISCILLA. You also can't undo God's omniscient plan.

AL. You can rely on your God or your science if you want, but I think the best place to locate my trust is in myself. I'm part of this natural order you talk about Charles and I plan to modify and manipulate it as much as possible to suit my needs,.. um and the needs of my constituents. (*He smiles at Amy. He hesitates a moment. Then turns and smiles at both Charles and Priscilla*).

AMY. We are freer and more important than you think, Charles. We the people make this existence that you claim controls us mean something more than just survival. We the people determine what's valuable in life and what isn't. We the people and not the law of the fittest decide who will be rich and successful and who will not. We even determine the definition of success and failure. And as far as God is concerned Priscilla, it is we the people who mold God into something understandable and useful.

AL. And it is this person, (*points to himself*), who is going to prevent Charles and Priscilla's so-called inevitable economic apocalypse. I might use taxation, regulation, inspiration, obfuscation, and yes, even necessary deception to do so. I'm not going to let people continue to suffer just because you two say they must.

FATHER. (*Smiles at Al*), I agree with Al in so far as Charles and Priscilla can not accurately predict anything with absolute confidence about the future. As I indicated earlier, the economic laws on which you base your predictions, Charles, are not really Darwin's but your own interpretation of them. Some might say that your interpretation relies as much on your own imagination and fantasies as you would say Amy's or Priscilla's do. If you really knew your Darwin as well as you think you do you would understand that Darwin saw evolution driven by more than mere survival

CHARLES. My understanding of Darwin is certainly better than yours.

FATHER. Then tell me how the huge and elaborate tail of the peacock helps it survive. It must surely slow it down when it tries to escape from predators.

CHARLES. The tail results from sexual selection. (*Amy looks up and smiles*). The bigger and more elaborate the tail the more likely the peacock will find a mate and reproduce. The more likely he reproduces the more likely that his genes and his big tail will survive into future generations. This means the fittest genes will survive.

FATHER. Yet the tail also makes it more likely he will be eaten before he can reproduce. The tail also means that his genes are less likely to survive.

CHARLES. Peacocks don't have that many predators, and obviously the added attractiveness of the feathers to a potential mate outweighs the survival disadvantages of the tails size. If not, there would be no peacocks with big tails left. Survival is still the ultimate outcome of the tail.

AMY. I'm surprised in you Charlie. It's so unlike you to recognize the power of sex and beauty. I agree with Daddy. I know from personal experience that both are very powerful and need to be reckoned with. Darwin might not have been such a dunce after all. Life is not just about doing something that makes us survive. Most of what you have had to say today looks very ugly. Beauty and passion should have a role in any economic solution too, and that's why I know your law of the fittest solutions won't work. Al if you really want to improve our economic life, don't forget to include something beautiful in your solutions.

AL. I'm way ahead of you Amy.

CHARLES. Beauty, must less sexual selection, has nothing to do with economics. It's absurd for you to think that you can improve an economy by making it look prettier.

FATHER. I wouldn't be so sure. The appearance of supply and demand may be just as important as the substance of the real supply and demand.

CHARLES. Give me an example.

FATHER. When a store persuades its customers that a product is popular, and might soon sell out, the demand for the product may increase substantially. It doesn't really matter if the original demand was true or not. Here the store creates the demand by making the product more desirable.

CHARLES. You've seen this happen?

AMY. Pet rocks.

PRISCILLA. Expensive vodka and other expensive liquor that tastes the same as the cheaper brands.

AL. Political candidates. Everyone wants to support a winner.

FATHER. If investors believe that others possess confidence in a company they will be more likely to invest their money in it even when they don't originally share that confidence.

AL. Yes, making an economic situation look beautiful and healthy might almost be as important as its true health and vitality.

CHARLES. The size and condition of the peacocks tail is a result of the animal's true health and vitality. It doesn't cause it. You can't just paste makeup on the face of an aging, sick economy and expect anyone to fall in love with it.

AL. If the old girl looks good, maybe someone will come along and buy her dinner. She will become a little healthier once she's well fed.

AMY. You said yourself that communism was a pretty ugly system and look what happened to it.

CHARLES. Capitalism outgrew and out survived Communism, because it was a more fit economic system and not because it was the most superficially pretty one.

FATHER. For the time being that might be true. That is, if we only use your definition of "fit", but if economies evolve the way you says species evolve, won't capitalism eventually be replaced by a fitter economic system.

AL. How can that be? Since competition forms the very basis of both capitalism and evolution, doesn't this mean that capitalism is best suited to deal with any evolutionary changes? By definition isn't capitalism and evolution pretty much the same thing? Doesn't capitalism ensure that only the "fittest" businesses will continue to evolve and grow the economy?

FATHER. Maybe not. Though capitalism has been very successful in promoting growth and has replaced several less efficient economic systems, better ways to operate an economy may well develop and replace it in turn. It has identified the potential demand of various goods and services better than any other system, and has utilized methods of production that other economic systems overlooked, but as it wears out these insights and methods, as it depletes resources, saturates markets, and lowers the cost of production to the point where insufficient profits or earnings can occur, it will reach a point where it can no longer expand the economy. Doesn't natural selection begin to work its magic most when a living thing fills its niche to its maximum carrying point, or when its environment changes?

CHARLES. (*Nods his head*). Something might replace capitalism eventually, but there's no reason to change course right now.

FATHER. How do you know that an immediate collapse won't occur in the near future? When capitalist economies eventually fail, couldn't they experience a sudden, total extinction rather than stagger along maintaining a muted level of economic activity until a more "fit" economic system slowly develops to replace it? Don't relatively sudden extinctions occur in nature? Doesn't evolution allow a rapid replacement of species less able to adapt as well as a more gradual replacement? Am I correct Charles?

CHARLES. (*Nods in agreement.*) Both occur but...

FATHER. Don't you think Al should be making plans should this ever happen to capitalism?

AL. (*Looks worried.*) Where is Capitalism in this evolutionary process? Am I trying to deal with the possible collapse of an economy, its long drawn out death or an early stage of economic growth? Can I grow the economy using capitalist tools a bit longer or should I turn away from capitalism to follow some new, "fitter" approach?

FATHER. That's the difficult question, isn't it? Do you continue to reap the benefits of capitalism or do you change it to adapt to new economic conditions? (*Al looks to his father in expectation*). I don't know the answer. You'll have to figure it out for yourself.

CHARLES. (*Leans back in his chair with his hands behind his head while grinning at Al, he begins to pontificate*). I like where you've gone with this father. Al might be able to squeeze a little more growth out of the economy using capitalism, but the inflated costs of both raw materials and labor, coupled with an increase in the world population and the economic expectations of this population tell me that if the system doesn't suddenly collapse in war or economic chaos it will only manage to produce a long steady stumble of economic stagnation. More to the point, there's no way you're going to survive the political carnage that will result from this state of affairs, (*Charles smiles gleefully*). Call me a pessimist, especially about your political prospects.

PRISCILLA. It's this god of competition that you and Al both revere that will cause this collapse and presently causes all the suffering I've seen in this world. This competition is an evil and destructive god. (*Amy nods in agreement*). Better to follow my God. There is no competition in my Kingdom of God.

CHARLES. (*Abruptly changes his grinning demeanor*). This kingdom of god of yours exists only in your imagination. Competition lives everywhere. I believe that you and your followers currently compete for your god's favor against the rest of us, the winners of this competition gaining the brass ring of the kingdom of god you fantasize about. Isn't that right? (*Priscilla nods 'yes' before catching herself*), And as far as the world where we're holding this conversation right now, look around you, everything, from microbes to microbiologists competes in one way or another.

AL. Priscilla, I need economic solutions for the here and now. Your Kingdom of God might solve all economic problems for a few people some day, but I'm not running for office in the Kingdom of God, and most of my constituents won't be residing there anyway.

AMY. We don't have to wait for Priscilla's solution to help and love each other. We don't have to die, or wait for an apocalypse. We can do it right now. In fact now is the best and only time to do it. We just have to decide to love rather than compete and fight each other.

CHARLES. Competition is everywhere. It flavors everything. You can't escape it. All cooperation ends in either chaos or competition. Even in a communist society, sectors of the economy competed for available resources, and in a socialist economy, you have to add in the competition between the government and everyone else for available resources. When there isn't enough to go around, people will always end up competing, and fighting.

AMY. That wouldn't happen in the economy I propose because the government wouldn't make people do anything they didn't want to do. Instead, people who had a lot would voluntarily share their resources with the needy.

AL. Not everyone would be willing to do that Amy. You would end up with a society where some people would share while others would continue to compete for whatever is available.

CHARLES. Those who share will not stand a chance against those who compete. The competitors would view them as weak, and take advantage of them. That is a natural fact.

AL. I'm afraid he's right Amy. The Easter Bunny would never stand a chance against the Big Bad Wolf, now would she?

AMY. Um, I've met plenty of big bad wolves, and I'm still around. A little tattered perhaps, (*Priscilla nods her head.*), but I somehow always manage to survive.

AL. There is an underlying implication to the phrase "the survival of the fittest" which is not clearly stated in the phrase itself, but which gives it much of its power and attraction.

FATHER. Which is?

AL. It's good to survive. Being alive and sentient and experiencing life is better than the nothingness of extinction. If survival is good so is being "the fittest". Perception may mold a great deal of the meaning of economic laws but some objective aspects of these laws must exist beyond the human imagination. Remember, if you don't survive, you can't perceive. I now agree with Charles. The need to survive is the basis of everything, which, of course, includes any economic solution I can think up.

FATHER. Survival is indeed important. It's the definition of fittest that is in question. If we could somehow separate the sharers and the competitors into separate societies, Amy's group of sharers might survive just as successfully as the competitors. Anthropologists have discovered several isolated societies who prospered by sharing everything.

CHARLES. Yes, and several inefficient animal species, like the Dodo have survived in isolation because they experienced no competition for resources, but outside species always eventually intrude, and this unexpected competition always leads to their extinction. We were the Dodo's unexpected competition when we invaded the Dodo's territory and destroyed them because they were easy to kill and tasted good.

PRISCILLA. The Dodo's downfall came in the form of greedy humans who consciously chose to be rapacious beasts. When capitalism operates without Christian values it becomes nothing more than any other invasive species. It finds a niche that offers little competition or other controls and quickly expands destroying whatever economic peace and stability existed there before. Make capitalism function with Christian values and you might fix our economic problems,

CHARLES. Your Christian values of lock step cooperation would stifle competition and be the ruin of capitalism.

FATHER. Cooperation by the kind of people who form the basis of Amy's economy has often improved their survivability, and occasionally, even increased their wealth. If cooperation causes a group to survive even a little while longer than they would have otherwise, doesn't this, according to your view make them fitter than a group that immediately disintegrates through constant infighting?

CHARLES. Cooperation can work only for a brief moment. You need to take a longer view, We must reject any economic system that eventually lessons a group's chances of survive We cannot consider it "the fittest" if it is susceptible to future disintegration when confronted with a more competitive and fit economy.

FATHER. No economic system is perfect, or can last forever. There are limits to how long term a view you can take to determine what is fit and what is not. Think of all those dinosaurs that were the fit survivors for millions of years, and are now extinct. The establishment of trade and cities required a great deal of human cooperation. All economic systems require such cooperation, particularly. Do you really believe that London or Venice could have ever been established by roving thugs and bandits who routinely preyed on each other in unchecked competition?

CHARLES. Both London and Venice were fierce competitors with other trading cities, and sometimes acted in a similar fashion to a thug or bandit, by making war and taking what they needed.

FATHER. Yet, within their own economy they encouraged cooperation among their citizens. I don't believe that we should ignore the value of Amy's propos Like the law of supply and demand, competition may indeed play an important role in every economy, but its opposite, cooperation does too. I'm just unwilling to give competition the sole authority over all economic transactions that you give it Charles.

PRISCILLA. The only authority we should acknowledge is the authority of God, and the rules he has set for us.

FATHER. I agree only to the extent that your god seems to want us to all cooperate and share. In the earliest Christian churches worship involved the sharing of a me I see this as the basis for your religion Priscilla, and not the eventual punishment of sinners as you seem to believe. To me, Christianity wants us to base our economic decisions on human needs and desires, and not on economic theories, or so-called Darwinian economic laws that deny their human antecedents or their subjective vindictiveness. The most robust economic systems must wear a human face, and preferably a smiling one.

AL. I can provide our economy with a smiling face Pops, I just need to know how much of Capitalism's bias toward free competition I should retain in my new, improved economic system. Do you believe that competition can continue to produce the economic growth we need or do you believe that I should start capping competition as soon as possible?

FATHER. Some competition will always prove useful in an economy, and as Charles indicated, you'll never be able to completely control it anyway. There are, however, a number of ways for an economy to grow that don't involve unrestricted competition. As you indicated earlier, an economy can grow simply by moving money faster and faster from person to person. Money that sits in a person's pocket does nothing to make an economy grow, but each economic transaction increases the size of the economy and the general feeling of wealth and economic well-being. Charles has said so himself.

CHARLES. It's still a zero sum game. One party has more money and the other has less after each economic transaction takes place.

FATHER. Both parties feel wealthier. One party now has the additional money he was seeking while the other has the product he wanted. Both have reason to feel satisfied. They both feel like winners. A financial transaction isn't always a zero sum struggle for wealth; most often it's a form of cooperation.

CHARLES. Both parties may feel better off, but no new wealth has been created for the economy as a whole. If the product is worth the price, the two parties have only exchanged two items of equal value. No new wealth has entered into the economy.

AL. (*As if seeing the light at the end of his political tunnel*). However, the item being sold didn't cost the seller as much as the buyer is paying for it. The seller is wealthier as a result, and since the buyer believes the item is worth what he paid for it, (he wouldn't buy it otherwise), he doesn't feel any poorer. He feels he possesses the same wealth he had before the transaction. The overall "feeling" of wealth of the economic community has increased. (He looks over at Amy). This almost feels like sharing doesn't it Amy?

AMY. Yes, it feels like the buyer and the seller are helping each other. I like that! Wealth isn't the dollars and cents printed on some bank statement. It is an experience of well being, isn't it? The expectation of the happiness a purchase will bring me creates some of its value of each economic transaction. In this manner satisfaction forms a necessary ingredient of all economies. All the statistics that economists produce by counting sales figures and bank deposits tell us very little about how much real wealth exists because they ignore this satisfaction. They're trying to count something that can't be counted, the feeling of satisfaction that we anticipate from buying and selling. If you can increase that sense amongst us, you will have solved a large part of our economic problems,

CHARLES. An increase in the feeling of wealth is not the same thing as the objective knowledge of an increase in goods and services. We base wealth on this knowledge and not a feeling.

AL. I wouldn't be too sure Charles. The gross national product of any country is a measurement of all its economic transactions as a whole. That's a lot of measurement, and much of it is a guess, or the result of sloppy measurement. Right Pops?

FATHER. Perhaps...though the problem we have in comprehending the sum and substance of our nation's wealth isn't just a matter of sloppy measurement. Some have defined wealth as a sheer abstract belief experienced in numbered units: the metal and paper faces of mutual trust. For example, Julian Bell has said that it is "a nothing and yet an everything, an almighty it, and at the same time, a storm of desire to embrace something we feel but don't completely understand - perhaps the fullness of the world." How can we measure something that we can barely define?

AL. I know wealth when I see it Pops. I can tell if one town is wealthier than another just by walking around and looking at the people, their houses and businesses. I don't need to use any of Charles' mathematical measurements

CHARLES. No wonder you're constantly in trouble. To properly manage an economy you need to utilize more precise methods than you're obviously capable of handling.

FATHER. There is more than one way to define wealth. Al's methods might sometimes work just as well as your measurements.

PRISCILLA. Wealth only exists when we build something worthwhile. The value of a product increases as a result of the thought and labor that goes into its making. I don't see Al taking any of that into consideration when he determines who is wealthy and who is not. Only work increases the value of the world we live in: work and moral uprightness.

CHARLES. I'm surprised you've managed to make any room at all for material wealth in this world. You do then acknowledge that wealth involves the creation of material products?

PRISCILLA. I only know how important material goods can become in the short term when trying to keep my flock fed while we wait for the coming Kingdom of God.

CHARLES. I will agree with you to the extent that, yes, we need dedicated workers to produce wealth, but I'd like to point out that capital is also a necessary ingredient of wealth creation. Without capital, investors have little opportunity to purchase and utilize the machinery, marketing, labor and transport needed for them to produce goods and services.

PRISCILLA. The most necessary ingredient in the production of material things is the labor of devoted, disciplined workers. God will take care of the rest of our needs. A good worker can make or find tools, and a good salesman will find a way to sell the product all with God's help.

CHARLES. We don't live in the Stone Age, and most of the time the maker and the seller of a product are two different people. Someone must pay both the maker and the seller with previously acquired capital before a sale can occur.

PRISCILLA. Usury only undermines morality. I agree with you only in that this world possesses no more value than that contained in its substance. Which is next to nothing. Any feeling of wealth this world might produce is an evil illusion. I find the material world necessary, but not particularly valuable in itself as you do. What increase the value of this world and its economy is human effort, proper conduct, and faith in God, (*She stares sternly at her father.*), none of these exist simply as a feeling. I have observed and weighed all of them, and if people do not live righteously and work diligently, as many do not, (*She glances over at Amy and Al*), then their moral worth will never increase. Their lives will become empty, and their true wealth will disappear. A 'feeling' of wealth or economic health will never solve our problems. Forget about increasing society's economic health through your lies and political tricks Al, or through your profit motivated investments Charles. These will only create the illusion of a good economy. If you want to solve our country's economic problems you've got to make people work, and live God fearing lives. Find a way to do that Al, and all our problems will be solved.

AL. You're talking about forced labor Priscilla? I don't see how this sets our economy free, or inspires economic growth.

PRISCILLA. Yes, if that's what it takes to make us worthy of economic success. Some sinners remain stubbornly attached to their idleness and sin. You must force them to work because they won't do so on their own. If they won't work, don't pay or feed them.

AMY. Forced labor is even more cruel and heartless than Charles' laissez faire survival of the fittest policy. You want to intentionally starve people you don't respect while Charles only wants to step out of the way and let them suffer.

CHARLES. Forced labor rarely results in the high output of quality products. Sometimes the results are so shoddy, that they are almost useless, at least they are here on earth Priscilla. Our experience with both Communism and slavery indicates as much, and shoddy products never form the satisfactory building blocks for a prosperous society or a healthy economy.

AMY. Maybe people will happily kneel to the authority of your Kingdom of God after they're dead, but we live ones won't.

FATHER. I fear your disdain of human weakness has caused you to lose sight of some of the most important aspects of your religion. As I recall, Jesus and the early Christians placed a great importance on feeding the hungry no matter how despised they were. Your brand of Christianity seems to be following a very different path.

PRISCILLA. (*Thinks a moment, and then looks up over everyone's head*). Maybe so, but I've seen my sister leave my church to hang out with her slacker friends, one brother lie and trick me into supporting him while he is simultaneously stabbing me in the back with legislation, and my other brother mocking everything I value and believe. You have all turned your back on me, and I reject all of you in return. Only God stands by my kind and me. I embrace his love and the beautiful future he promises. I loathe this world and all the sinners in it. If I've rejected Jesus mercy, it is you who have driven me to do so.

AMY. I haven't turned my back on you Priscilla. I'd stand by you if you weren't continually judging every little thing I do or think. I stopped attending your church because you were constantly making an example of me to your parishioners. Those friends of mine who you dislike so much don't do that. They like me. We don't try to put ourselves above each other. We know we are all in the same leaky boat and that we will have to take turns keeping it afloat. So far we have been able to do so. We could use more of Al's help though. I have a few ideas you might want to consider

AL. (*Nods to Amy*). Of course, I'm always glad to hear your ideas. (*Turns to Priscilla*). Perhaps your congregation is ready to embrace some overwhelming authority, but my constituents are not. There has to be a give and take between leaders and the led. I need choices and so do they. Come to think of it, that is one reason to retain Capitalism. Capitalism fosters more choices. Under it people have more choice about what to buy and where to work. This kind of flexibility has proven to be very useful.

SUBSTANCE OR FEELING?
WHICH LEG IS STRONGER?

CHARLES. While I don't believe that we can practically implement Priscilla's notion that people should only be given the choice to work or eat. I hold no emotional biases against the idea. Unlike you and your "feelings" Amy, my logic and reason allows me to view Priscilla's forced labor proposal without complicating it with a lot of emotional baggage. Logic and reason can objectively measure the cost of this forced labor, in the same way it can the cost of natural resources, capital, and the unforced labor in a non slave economy. Logically labor is quite simply one of the inputs for the creation of wealth and economic growth, nothing more and nothing less. Labor is not one of your "feelings" which you vaguely think is important. Al, you must base any lasting economic solutions not on feelings, but on substance. Labor is a substance whether performed by slaves or free men.

FATHER. Substantial and measurable inputs to an economy have their place in understanding and fixing a dysfunctional economy, but you make a serious mistake when you ignore the intangible factors like subjective impressions that we must also consider when fixing an economy. Labor is much more than a measurable substance. The attitudes of managers and workers toward each other and toward themselves are hard to measure and yet mightily important to the success of an economy.

AMY. (*Nods*) Yes, the idea of labor should include cooperation, and even friendship. Labor involves relationships between people.

AL. There must also be an understanding of how labor can best generate quality products efficiently. This understanding must consider the feelings of individual workers. It must promote a desire, a feeling, on the part of workers to work with managers and investors rather than against them. This can occur only when workers feel that they are receiving a fair share of the economy's success. They must feel that it is their economy too, and that their standard of living will improve when their managers' and company's investors do.

PRISCILLA. (*Looking at Al*). Well, yes. The satisfaction of a job well done…that's important, as well as the understanding that God sanctifies their toil and approves their proper attitude toward work.

AL. Neither of which has ever occurred under forced labor, nor under any economic system that considers labor to be nothing more than a material to be used as cheaply as possible.

FATHER. I think we need to talk more about how immaterial factors determine a society's economic success. If we look closely at past long term solutions to previous economic crisis I believe we will see that subjective influences molded most of them at least as much as objective, material ones did.

CHARLES. We live in a materially finite world. Wealth can be created only when labor uses the materials from this finite world to make a needed product. Thus, finite substances have always formed the foundation of all economies. It's a reality no one can escape no matter what new way you want to look at it. For example we are currently depleting the earth's storehouse of fossil fuels. We are already burning fuel and dumping carbon into the atmosphere faster than plants can take it up and turn it back into fuel. When we finally run out of these fuels, most of world's economic production will cease and a serious economic collapse will result. (*He smiles and glances over at Al*).

FATHER. The earth's resources may be limited, but the possible use and reuse of these resources may be infinite. We can also extend them by adding the immaterial qualities that Al, Amy, and Priscilla find important. We may learn to see the world in new ways that will free up resources that we never previously knew existed.

AL. True enough, the amount of carbon-based fuels on the earth may be finite, but we might develop the capacity to change atmospheric carbon back to fuel.

FATHER. Unknown potentials have always surrounded us, and the uncertainty of our predicament focuses our attention in such a way that we may eventually find and use them. The human mind possesses a wonderful, almost magical facility in this regard. Humanity has proven repeatedly that it can overcome the perceived limitations of the material world.

CHARLES. The human mind is indeed a powerful problem-solving machine. I'll grant you that. I'm pleased that you've finally recognized the superior usefulness of mind and reason over the chaotic mess of emotion.

FATHER. I recognize no such thing. We need both emotion and reason to solve the problems that confront us. The foundations of the best solutions often lie in the obscure regions of human imagination and feeling as well as in rationality. We need to start looking in all three areas if we are ever to find the solutions to our economic problems.

CHARLES. That's nonsense. We need to base our solutions on substantial facts, not immaterial dreams. You make economic thought sound like pure fantasy

FATHER. It's not completely an illusion, but many economic "truths" rest on subjectivity to one degree or another. Facts and dreams can partly overlap each other and where they do, we can turn the results into the new truths of new solutions.

CHARLES. You don't create truth. You find it.

FATHER. Not only does substance, imagination, and emotion blend and separate again within economic theories, but over time imagination and emotion changes the very substance of whole economies. We here in the United States, for instance, now base our economy less on material substances and more on the immaterial products of emotion and imagination.

CHARLES. I need some solid examples of this transition for me to understand it.

FATHER. The first economic revolution occurred with the development of agriculture. Before this occurred, economies, such as they were, were very small and based on bartering products acquired through handicrafts, hunting or gathering. People lived on what they could find or make themselves. This economy supported human societies that were "nasty, brutish, and short". *(Thomas Hobbes). Given the limits imposed upon it by its physical environment it could never grow very large, and could support only a small number of people. This was a very problematic and inefficient economy. Many died of famine, and few, if any, could be considered prosperous. The agricultural revolution that occurred about 6,000 years ago changed the nature of this economy and humanity's quality of life substantially. As more and more people turned to agriculture for their livelihood, more and more food was produced. Food surpluses freed up some people to engage in other economic activities. Construction workers no longer had to spend time searching for food and could begin building temples and cities. Craftsmen could concentrate on making better and better goods that they could trade for food or for other goods from other craftsmen. With increased food production Cities could grow in size, and civilization began its slow rise. Human economies began to grow beyond their tiny beginnings. Trade became more than just a haphazard event. Economic growth had begun, and it felt good.

CHARLES. Yes, you've proved my point. Food is a substance. There is nothing immaterial about this economic revolution of agriculture.

FATHER. I agree. Though people had to apply a good deal of thought and discipline to create this evolution, its product is a substance, and a very necessary one. This is only the starting point of our journey of economic expansion, however.

CHARLES. So far we agree.

FATHER. The next economic revolution was the industrial revolution. People who could no longer find employment in farming...

CHARLES. (*Breaks in*). Because the amount of farmland was finite and limited.

FATHER. (*Nods*) ...moved to cities where capitalists employed them in newly designed factories where they produced manufactured goods more cheaply and efficiently than they did when they worked in cottage industries. The cheapness of these goods meant that people could afford to buy more of them, which, in turn, caused factories to employ more people to produce more goods to meet this demand. The world economy grew much larger and much faster than any agricultural/craft economy ever had before.

CHARLES. These mass produced products are still material, and now your economies are using more and more of the earth's finite resources.

You are simply proving my point. The world's economies hadn't become immaterial at all.

FATHER. In many respects, they had not, but in at least one respect, they had. The agricultural economies produced goods that people needed to survive. If there were no food, people would die. If a person did not have a single set of clothes, they might freeze to death during the winter. The industrial revolution produced more and more products that people wanted but didn't absolutely need if they were to survive. The products continued to be material, but the need for them less so. The need for the products of the industrial revolution became less and less substantial as more and more became available, even if the products themselves remained material objects. They became less and less a requirement for human existence and more and more a result of immaterial human vanity and desire.

CHARLES. You make a very fine distinction between the products of an agricultural economy and of an industrial one, but I grant you that they are not exactly the same in terms of their importance to continued human existence.

FATHER. Both the agricultural and industrial revolutions nurtured an increase in the human population. With this increase, more and more people found themselves temporarily or permanently unemployed. People were being born faster than the growing agricultural and manufacturing economies could absorb them. These economies also began to need fewer workers as competition between countries and rival businesses forced them to become more efficient. Economic depressions resulted. Countries fought wars to gain raw materials and markets for finished goods. People suffered, and many sought new economic solutions to bring them out of this misery. Philosophers like Malthaus thought that such economic solutions were impossible. He was wrong, Charles.

AMY. This actually happened? People starved to death or died in senseless wars? I'm glad I didn't live then. How did we fix this horrid economy Daddy? We must have done something right since we no longer live like those poor people did.

PRISCILLA. People still starve and die in senseless wars, Amy. As usual, you find ways to ignore the obvious suffering of others. (*Amy looks at her blankly.*)

FATHER. Services have always existed, probably even back to our hunter-gatherer days, but it wasn't until relatively recently that we saw that a good deal of unemployment could be absorbed and economies expanded through service jobs. Economists, the governments they advised, and workers themselves recognized that there was room for expanding the amount and type of services people could and would buy. As a result of their efforts by all three groups the service economy expanded exponentially. A large part of the labor force began to enter service jobs, until today the largest segment of the U.S. workforce relies on these jobs. Our economy and your way of life, Amy, rest squarely on these service jobs. We escaped the economic nightmare prophesized by Malthaus at least partly by cultivating a service economy.

CHARLES. Hmm, yes, Malthus. The service economy solution you're promoting appears pretty fragile to me. This type of economy could collapse if most people got sick in an epidemic. Economies built on the production of solid and necessary items like food or houses seems a lot more robust to me.

AMY. You're right Father. These services are very solid and important. I would be miserable if I couldn't get my hair done, and it's nice to know that I am keeping America economically strong whenever I do so. I'm a patriot Al!

CHARLES. I can see where this is going.

FATHER. Yes, the products of service employment are less physical, material, and substantive than manufactured products, Charles, but most services last only temporarily, and often have to be repeated over and over again. This repetition strengthens and grows the economy. It is less likely for an service economy to produce too many services than an industrial or agricultural economy is to produce too many material widgets, or food or whatever. For example, an agricultural economy may produce corn, which people can store for future consumption. When too much corn lies in storage, its price drops, farmers plant less of it and may lay off some of their workers. An industrial economy might produce hammers, which consumers do not replace until they lose or break them. When too many hammers are made and lie in inventory, the hammer factory may close down and lay off its workers. A service economy, on the other hand, may produce haircuts, which by their very nature cannot be stored up and must be repeated over and over again. It is much less likely that barbers will close up shop when they feel it's possible that a new customer may walk through the door at any moment.

CHARLES. Service economies still produce a number of physical artifacts though. Services produce deeds, insurance policies, and diplomas. I would argue that the new physical appearance we have after a haircut is a material outcome of the service. Solid products still matter most.

FATHER. There is a physical and material component to all these services, but we have moved a long way from an economy that produced the most basic and necessary materials needed for survival.

AL. The service economy has been in place for a long time. It has done a good job employing people, but like the other two economies, it's no longer absorbing as many people as it used to do. Where can I look for the next big economic movement that will give people work, create wealth, and help me out of the political quagmire where economics has dumped me?

PRISCILLA. Where you dumped yourself.

FATHER. Today we are using the digital economy to generate employment and economic growth. We do this by producing the most insubstantial products of all, information and entertainment. The only material artifact of this economy is the static electricity found on a DVD or computer screen. Ultimately, we are selling thought. For the most part, we do not need these products to survive. They do not even produce a service we really need. We are buying and selling products whose function is simply to make us happier and better informed.

AL. That sounds like your Kingdom of God Priscilla. (*Laughs*). Everyone is happy and has all the answers. Pops, this new economy is real enough to actually employ people, and generate the kind of wealth that people can spend, right?

CHARLES. I'm not sure it IS much more real than Priscilla's Kingdom of God. We may just be creating the illusion of wealth and prosperity. I think your analysis of the evolution of the world's economies supports my belief that we are all heading toward an economic collapse rather than economic salvation. After each economic crisis our economies changed to produce less substantial and necessary products. The economic changes you describe didn't create more robust economies but more and more insubstantial ones. We've come to a point now, where we are basing our economic health on almost nothing at all. The next great economic change, if it continues to evolve the way it has, will result in economic nothingness. Wealth will have no meaning. Labor will create nothing but empty dreams.

PRISCILLA. Now you see the light Charles. Everything you capitalists have created will simply evaporate and you will recognize it for the illusion that it is. Poverty and destitution will devour everyone alike here on earth. This end of days will leave only one hope for humankind, God's grace. A sea of darkness and violence will swamp those who don't put their faith in God.

CHARLES. I put my faith in no god of yours Priscilla. Civilization may wither away but a few bright islands of wealth and stability surrounded by the sea of darkness you rather accurately portray will continue. Civilization has survived some rough patches in the past. It will do so again.

FATHER. Who exactly would be living on these few bright islands?

CHARLES. People like me, who had looked ahead and took the appropriate steps for economic and physical survival: Intelligent, rational people, who know how to manage and control the material world.

FATHER. You make it sound like human thought creates and protects these islands of civilization and stability from the chaos that surrounds them, yet you earlier claimed that the thought that forms most of the product of the internet economy is mostly unsubstantial illusion. How do you resolve this contradiction? Are thoughts and ideas insubstantial illusions unconnected with the material "real" world or are they the one thing that will save the inhabitants of your islands of wealth and stability?

CHARLES. That depends on what you call ideas. Practical ideas support survival. Unsubstantial ideas do not. Practical ideas help us control and manipulate the real, physical world. The music and other fluff the Internet dangles before us offers nothing useful for survival, and the clearly erroneous ideas like Priscilla's kingdom of god eventually harm our chances of survival

AL. I think Charles might be right. The Internet economy won't save us because it often divides us into feuding groups that are less willing to address our common problems. Like Priscilla's Kingdom of God, the Internet allows people to see themselves as the righteous elect and everyone else as foolish knaves. For some reason I'm always being placed in the latter group. I'm sure you see how your bright islands would end up doing the same thing, can't you Charles?

CHARLES. (*Shrugs.*)

AMY. You're wrong. I find the Internet to be very important for my happiness and survival It tells me what the world offers beyond my own group of friends, and it entertains me when I feel low. It nourishes my soul Priscilla.

PRISCILLA. It provides nothing but deceit and temptation. It poisons the minds of those who are not wise enough to resist it.

AL. You've used it, Priscilla, to tell everyone how ineffective and wrong my policies have become. (*Sighs*). It seems to me that you engage in doling out poison as much as anyone else.

PRISCILLA. Sometimes you have to use questionable means to fight evil.

FATHER. That really doesn't sound like a policy that Jesus would condone, or follow himself.

CHARLES. Amy, like cotton candy, most of the content of the Internet may taste good, but it usually provides little if any rational nourishment when your survival is at stake. Only the detailed knowledge of science, technology and the other practical arts are worth sharing on the Internet. Only these aspects of civilization will help those of us who will survive a total economic collapse. These are the only parts of civilization that possess real substance and are worth saving.

FATHER. The civilization you intend to preserve on your islands would be pretty thin and bland without the sweet "fluff" you dismiss so easily.

AMY. My friendships with others have helped me the most to survive my unemployment, and lack of money. You don't seem to have many friends at the moment Charles. How will you survive without friends?

CHARLES. There will be like-minded individuals on these islands of reason and stability.

AL. That ought to work out well; a civilization composed of elitist prima donnas who each think they know the best and only way to get something done.

AMY. No one can survive without the help and emotional support of others. Your islands of knowledge seem pretty gray and grim to me. I'm not sure I'd want to survive in a world that didn't contain any of what you consider emotional nonsense. The Internet supports my friendships and human connections, and because of them I will survive a lot longer than you will with your reason and pragmatism.

CHARLES. The Internet has also caused unnecessary conflict and ignorance among your friends. I'm sure it's taught you that some of your friends aren't really your friends at all. The falsehoods it often dishes out are not always sweet and entertaining, are they?

AL. (*Nods in agreement*).

AMY. Maybe not, but I prefer to focus on the music, art and literature it delivers at the click of a little plastic mouse. I choose to ignore any of its ugly falsehoods, or any of its ugly truths for that matter.

CHARLES. Turning your back on the truth, no matter how ugly it might be, can only limit your ability to survive any coming disaster.

Amy I use the Internet to provide me with a happiness that ugly truths cannot. While I know we can't be happy if we don't survive, survival without happiness should not be a goal either. The purpose of civilization is happiness, not survival, and any modern economy should do more than allow a few people to survive by squirreling themselves away on a rock someplace. Al should design his economy to shower as much happiness as possible on as many people as possible. I think the Internet can help him do it.

FATHER. Whatever its consequences, the Internet economy does have a substance and usefulness even you can appreciate Charles. It advertises material products that people need and ultimately buy and use. It helps move physical products from one place to another by coordinating the movement of real trucks and real people. This increased efficiency reduces spoilage of food, that most basic of all products which played such a key role in the first economic revolution. The Internet economy also allows us to transmit information quickly from designers and managers to production lines so that workers can make appropriate products correctly. The electronic hardware that accompanies the Internet economy has subsequently multiplied small business's efficiency as much as the nuts and bolts machinery did during the industrial revolution. Finally, the Internet economy is not an illusion, because, it creates real wealth, for the rest of us to spend.

PRISCILLA. These electronic inventions are also much more dangerous than the old nuts and bolts machinery because they operate more covertly than steam engines or power looms did. The wealth and greed these new devices generate is less apparent, more easily hidden, and more difficult to mitigate and control.

AL. (*He raises his hand in the air.*) I pledge to regulate the Internet while supporting its expansion of the Internet if I am reelected! (*He nods to Priscilla.*)

AMY. (*Claps her hands.*)

CHARLES. All right, I admit that developing the Internet economy will help us in the short term, but eventually it will produce too much, and will suffer from the same sort of boom and bust syndrome every other type of economy has experienced. Eventually, it won't be able to grow fast enough to match population growth. Millions will end up unemployed, and national economies and social systems will crumble into chaos.

FATHER. If the products of human thought are infinite, Charles, then economic growth based on human thought could be infinite too. Don't you agree?

CHARLES. Even if human thoughts were infinite, and I don't know how you can prove it is, the space that encapsulates human thought is finite. The earth can support only a finite number of people. Your Internet might be able to provide employment to an expanding population for a while, though an economy where billions of people are selling ideas and music to each other seems a bit far-fetched, but the Internet will not be able to feed or house them. No matter how efficient the Internet may make agriculture, forestry and mining, eventually the earth will not be able to provide the necessary resources for all the products these participants will need to survive in this Internet economy. As resources become scarcer they will also become more expensive. People won't be able to earn enough from the Internet economy to pay for what they need. Al and his ilk may print more currency in the vain hope that people can use it to pay for the more expensive products, but this will only drives prices higher. No one can make a profit by making products that no one can afford to buy. Web sites will close. People will be laid off. We could face the untenable position of experiencing inflation and depression simultaneously. This will constitute an almost total economic Armageddon. (*He grins again in Al's direction*)

AL. (*Takes a deep breath.*)

PRISCILLA. (Also smiles).

FATHER. Your economic end of days, Charles, might occur if no one does anything to avoid it, (He glances meaningfully over at Priscilla). No one with a conscience could simply sit back and watch all the suffering and possible death such a disaster would create and not try to do something about it. Someone might find a way to head it off. (*Al clears his throat and smiles at everyone*).

AMY. We might avoid such awful times through music.

(*Father looks thoughtful while the rest smile in amusement*).

AMY. Daddy when you talked about the value of beauty reviving an economy I thought you were talking about more than the perception that the economy is healthy. I thought you meant that beautiful things actually improve an economy.

CHARLES. More nonsense.

AMY. It isn't! Daddy once told me that the beautiful music of the Beatles once helped save the British economy.

FATHER. They were knighted for their work. The Second World War had almost bankrupted Great Britain. It struggled through the late 40's and the 50's to just barely keep its head above water. It tried both capitalist and socialist modeled initiatives to reinvigorate economic life, but nothing seemed to work for nearly a whole generation. The music of the Beatles and other British groups suddenly became very popular worldwide, particularly in the United States. This popularity created a great demand for this type of music and large amounts of cash began to flow into the British economy. The British music invasion of the United States produced the income that Great Britain needed to raise its citizen's standard of living. Life became less of a struggle, and material goods became more affordable after the British music industry took off.

CHARLES. There were a lot of other influences on the British economy at that time too. Your thesis ignores them. The growth of the British financial services industry has also played a role in the improvement of the overall British economy. This occurred because the industry was much less fettered with regulations there than on the continent. Another example where less regulation helped create a better economy. Looser regulations made the British financial industry the dominating survivor it is today.

FATHER. I see some truth in that, but the cash that flowed into government and private coffers as a result of the cultural success of the British music industry provided a lot of the cash that primed the pumps of the British financial services industry's success. Without the first success, the second might not have ever occurred.

CHARLES. I think you would have a hard time proving your theory. Remember, no one can prove a negative. The laws of logic prevent it. You should place your faith in economic facts that can be substantiated, Al, when you set out to fix the economy, rather than entering some economic beauty pageant.

FATHER. You have a subjective attitude too that you can't seem to see. You call your perceptions, "facts". If you insist on calling them facts you should call them "facts for the moment".

CHARLES. I can measure and quantify my facts. You can do neither with your unsubstantial speculations about the influence of music on the British economy? That's the difference between you and me. I can prove what I say. You can't.

FATHER. My perceptions also involve facts: I can compute the number of Beatle records sold between 1968 and 1972. I can determine how much profit was earned from these sales. I can locate how much the Beatles and the record companies paid in income taxes for those years.

CHARLES. Sure you can, and I can produce a number for how much the British GDP increased or decreased during those years, and I can show that the sales of Beatles records and the increase of GDP are not the same numbers. The increase of the taxes collected from the Beatles, and other groups, also does not equal any decrease in the British national debt. Your numbers prove nothing.

FATHER. How can you say that the cash generated by this music didn't improve the British economy? It must have had some effect. How could it have been a negative influence? No matter how much economic data we collect we can never be sure that either one of us has gathered enough to justify a final judgment. If we required absolute proof of everything, we would never believe anything. We would never do anything, *(Lee Smolin) and the complete objectivity you ascribe to the exact sciences is a delusion and false ideal *(Michel Polanyi) Sometimes you just have to make a leap of faith.

CHARLES. Such leaps often lead people off in the wrong direction.

FATHER. Yes, and so does relying just on data. Data is also as subject to error and human manipulation as faith is. It reflects the past rather than the murky future and currently "unseen" conditions. We can often interpret hard data in several ways according to our preformed ideas about what constitutes an "economic law". We often hide our emotions and subjectivity behind facts simply to win an argument by appearing objective. Attitudes and imperfect perceptions lie beneath a lot of economic thought. Facts, of course, exist, but they are often marinated in emotion and subjectivity before we use them. We would be more honest if we admitted this and consciously accepted that we build attitudes and subjective perceptions into our economic decisions rather than claiming that we rely solely on "objective" facts.

CHARLES. An economic system can be understood only through cold hard facts. We build all economies, even Socialist ones like Amy's 'economy of sharing' out of facts and not out of human perceptions or 'feelings".

AL. Humans are the measuring device as well as the measurer. Without people your facts and the reality they purport to measure remain meaningless and hold no value. Your facts are nothing without the "you" to create them through some measurements that "you" or someone like you devised and a "you" to make some sort of sense out of them. Existence has value only to the extent that humans can perceive, describe, and understand what it is. The amount of money in circulation, existing interest rates, profit and loss, supply and demand all hold little value in any existence where people haven't already created and manipulated these ideas.

PRISCILLA. Wait a minute. That's not....

FATHER. (*Breaks in quickly*). Economies are built out of how people perceive your so-called facts. I'm sure you can come up with a number that describes our money supply, but it is no more than an educated guess, and different economists will interpret the significance of the number differently, because even those most dedicated to the truth disagree about which truths matter. *(Geoffrey Hawthorn)

CHARLES. It's not an educated guess. We know exactly how much currency and credit the Treasury and the Federal Reserve Bank have put into the economy.

FATHER. How much currency was lost or destroyed last year? How much sits forgotten in someone's safe deposit box rather than in circulation? Did you deduct the amount given to the skyjacker DW Cooper?

CHARLES. Why should I?

FATHER. They found some of it in the forest where he bailed out. He might have died, and the money might be rotting somewhere on the forest floor. The bills given to him have never surfaced in circulation. Do you include this money in your money supply data ?As far as your accurate credit data is concerned, many people apply for credit and then never use it, or they die and their spouse never knows that it exists. Does credit exist if the person possessing it doesn't know it exists, and never uses it? Your "facts" about the money supply and credit aren't facts at all, but rough guesses.

CHARLES. All right. So economists use rounded approximate numbers. The amounts involved are so large that small inaccuracies don't matter.

FATHER. Small inaccuracies in the "facts" found on a company's balance sheet and income statement can matter when a company's management uses them to tell a story favorable to the company. The public's perception of the "facts" reflected in these "objective" reports can increase the value of a company's stock quite a bit.

CHARLES. If the data is "massaged" according to generally accepted accounting rules, then any misperceptions are the faults of the persons reading the report. If he or she read it carefully and correctly they would have an accurate picture of the company's success or failure.

PRISCILLA. If the data is "massaged" in violation of these rules, are they still facts? If not, what should we call them?

FATHER. Do you think economists study every company's financial reports to determine the "facts" of a company's profit and loss and whether or not they scrupulously followed accounting rules before compiling their Gross National Product reports or even their understanding of a general industry's profit and loss?

CHARLES. No, but again the inaccuracies reported by one company are averaged away by the accurate reports of many other companies. GNP, money supply, credit utilization, these reports all deal with large numbers that are still meaningful, even if a little inaccurate.

FATHER. Where do you draw the line between "facts" that are close enough and incorrect data? When various small inaccuracies pile up, at what point do they begin to mislead economists? It seems to me that your "facts" aren't rock solid after all.

CHARLES. My facts are a lot more permanent and useful than your emotional perceptions. A reality exists beyond your biased and subjective perceptions; facts and unerring truths have a home in this reality.

AMY. Where is this reality? If it's not here and now, describe it for me.

CHARLES. It can't be described because it exists beyond the artifice of human language. It exists whether people exist to experience it or not. It's older and more permanent than humanity. It is eternal.

PRISCILLA. AMEN!

AMY. (*Giggles*).

FATHER. Such a reality might very well exist, but perceptions have an intimate relationship with your facts that you can never sever, and often play a larger role in economic success than the facts do. This is especially true when timing economic decisions. For example, a government may report a large balance of payments deficit, but the public may ignore this fact for years before they actually react to this information. Their currency will remain stable, and interest rates will remain low despite economic theories that predict that a trade deficit will have the opposite effect. The United States carried a huge balance of payments deficit for years without affecting its currency or interest rates in any meaningful way. People can ignore facts for a very long time, and then react to them for some purely emotional reason.

AMY. Why is that?

CHARLES. People focus their attention erratically. Often they don't want to see the facts that lie plainly before them. So they don't. This state of affairs never lasts forever. Eventually, people will understand the importance of facts and act on this importance.

FATHER. True. Nothing continues forever, Charles, not even the facts you think are apparent and completely understood. Human perceptions change, sometimes quite suddenly. A vague, fuzzy notion that has always been lying a bit out of focus in the background can jump into our center of attention and replace what we had previously accepted as a "fact", as the new fact. At other times the 'facts' on which people have based their understandings aren't immediately replaced but fade slowly away. These facts eventually become perceived as illusions. They are illusions, however, that possess very real consequences before, during, and after their lives as facts, because when the group's illusions change, their economic realities change. Currencies may become worthless, interest rates may sky rocket, stock markets may crash, and businesses may shut down. The public may perceive these changes as necessary and inevitable, or as a huge misunderstanding. The impetus behind these perceptions may be real or imagined issues. The facts you rely on so much Charles, are as fluid as water.

CHARLES. Yet the facts can be described much more clearly than these perceptions you speak of. When a company announces that its earnings have dropped ten cents from the previous year, it is usually true and its meaning clear. Usually the price of the stock will drop in a rational manner. The company earns less so the company is worth less. One fact logically leads to another.

FATHER. It's probably worth less, unless there is some new product in the pipeline that few people know about yet, or unless a major competitor is having bigger troubles that haven't come to light yet. In such cases your company's stock may really be worth more. You may never have enough available facts to determine the true value of the company's stock. The stock's value ultimately rests on other investor's subjective impressions of the company, not some objective 'fact'.

CHARLES. Other investors' subjective perceptions and feelings taken as a whole can be considered a fact. That is what the charts I follow are all about. They objectively chart investor's attitudes and feelings about individual stocks or about the market as a whole. These charts can predict much about the value of a particular stock, or of the stock market as a whole.

AMY. You're always saying I'm foolish because I make my decisions according to how I feel. When you use these charts to predict the future, you're making decisions based on the feelings of people you don't even know.

CHARLES. Economists have discovered that human emotions exhibit predictable patterns over the long run. I follow these predictable patterns as they are reflected in stock prices.

FATHER. If a stock's price is shown to cross over its 120-day average price line, what does that mean to you?

CHARLES. The stock's price will rise.

FATHER. Why do you believe that?

CHARLES. The chart shows that people are becoming more and more optimistic about the future success of the company and the value of its stock. They believe that the price of the stock is likely to continue to rise and they will buy more. The price will continue to rise as a result.

FATHER. But the people who buy this stock based on the chart are not really making logical, rational decisions, are they? They are not buying the stock because there is hard evidence that the stock is undervalued. They are buying it because a lot of other people are buying it. They get caught up in the buying emotions of a lot of other flawed and emotional humans. They "feel" the stock price will continue to rise, right?

CHARLES. Yes, but I'm charting those feelings objectively, and making a prediction based on how people have reacted in these kinds of situations in the past. These charts rarely let me down.

AL. I wonder if "rarely" means the same to you that it does to me. Also, isn't it possible that people buy more of a stock when its price goes above that 120-day average line, because people like you have told them that the chart proves that the price will continue to go up? We politicians successfully use that form of influencing all the time.

CHARLES. Unlike you, we seek to reveal the truth.

FATHER. You claim that we must prevent emotion from ever sullying our objectivity. You also claim that you rely only on objective facts and reason when using these charts advice to buy and sell stocks. Am I right?

CHARLES. Absolutely.

FATHER. The people's behavior you are charting might be making incorrect, emotionally biased decisions. Am I correct to assume that?

CHARLES. Yes

FATHER. Then how can you rely on their mistaken perceptions to make what you think is an objective decision? You are tapping into second hand emotions while convincing yourself that you are using an objective method. Making decisions based on emotions that are not even your own seems to me to make your decisions even more uncertain. In addition to this, you seem to have an emotional attachment to your charts, which according to you should make your objective use of them even more unlikely.

AMY. You believe in these charts only because you can see them and they have the appearance of being objective. This appearance allows you to place enough faith in them for you to make sense out of them, a sense that may or may not be true. I do the same thing when I begin a new relationship. Neither you nor I can be completely objective about something we already believe; it's humanly impossible. So why pretend to try? We might as well do what we do best. Which is to feel our way through life. Your objective natural laws that you claim control all economic life are just something that someone made up to explain events that may or may not have occurred in the past. We feel we need explanations for these events and we do the best we can to create some that **feel** reasonable.

Your belief in economic natural laws is no more objective than Priscilla's understanding about Adam Smith's invisible hand of god, nor in what I might understand about a new boyfriend.

CHARLES. And no more so than your misguided belief in the all-powerful benefits of love and cooperation. When the next economic collapse occurs your chances of survival won't be much better than the dodo's was.

AL. If you believe that a total economic collapse is inevitable, then your scientific research business won't be much help to you. Stocks, bonds, even cash won't help you survive. You'll be in the same precarious situation as Amy. She might actually survive longer than you since I'm sure people would rather have her around than you. Why do you believe that your survival in an economic collapse will be any more guaranteed than that of Amy and her circle of friends?

THE GOLDEN RULE?

CHARLES. I've invested most of the profit from the sale of my patents in gold and silver bullion. These will retain their value even in the worst of times.

AL. (*Surprised*). You didn't reinvest your profits back into your new business?

CHARLES. No I sought out a less risky investment.

AL. (*Smiles to himself*).

AMY. What makes you think gold and silver aren't risky investments?

PRISCILLA. It figures that you would take your thirty pieces of silver as your wages of sin.

CHARLES. Gold and silver are solid, material objects of wealth. They have always been valuable, and will continue to be when all other forms of wealth have withered away. Father might be correct to say that part of the value of various financial instruments and of currency itself rests on people's subjective perceptions. These perceptions, while somewhat illusionary, have a purpose as long as an economy rolls along. They become simply figments of the imagination, however, when an economy collapses. Gold and silver are real material objects. Unlike stocks, bonds, and currency you cannot create gold and silver out of thin air. The human imagination cannot create these. They must be found and dug out of the ground. For this reason there will always be a limited supply and they will always have value. When you print more money or issue more stocks and bonds their value can decline. Theoretically there are no limits to the amount of stock certificates, currency, or debt that can be issued. During a financial meltdown the illusionary nature of these financial instruments can be recognized and their value can plummet.

AL. If the kind of apocalyptic collapse you predict actually occurs, I don't see what good gold and silver will do you. As Pizarro learned you can't eat it.

CHARLES. No but I can trade it for food, clothing and other necessities because these precious metals will always have value.

FATHER. They are valuable only as long as other people think they are valuable. Their value is as much an illusion as the value of paper financial instruments. These metals have little practical use in themselves except as the material to fabricate pretty things. Your financial apocalypse, if it becomes as bad as you think, might convince people that such baubles are trivial and unnecessary. People might trade food and crafts directly. would be extinct in such an environment, so you wouldn't have much of an opportunity to use these metals as capital either. Even without such an apocalyptic scenario, the value of gold and silver has declined many times in the past as the public's attitude toward them changed.

CHARLES. Even when gold's value dropped, it never went to zero, because the amount of gold in the world is limited. This limited supply will always factor into the supply/demand calculation of its value.

FATHER. The demand side of that calculation remains as uncertain as ever. The demand for gold is nothing more than a fickle human desire.

Its value could go to zero if people suddenly decided they didn't like the way it looked, and recognized that everyone else felt the same way. Just because something is rare doesn't mean that it is valuable. Van Gogh's paintings are rare and valuable today, while they were just as rare but not very valuable when he died. He only managed to sell two in his lifetime, and they were both to his brother. During an economic apocalypse his art might again become worth next to nothing.

AL. True, and if gold does maintain its value in an economic meltdown it's unlikely that you could go to a store and buy a quart of milk and loaf of bread with it. (He laughs.), or for that matter, with a Van Gogh if it has retained its value. The value of these rare items would probably be too large for small purchases.

CHARLES. You might be able to use silver coins for small purchases.

FATHER. With which you might have the same problems that people have had with silver coins in the past. Coins will be clipped, melted down, adulterated and recast as the originals. These practices will cause the value of the coins to drop.

CHARLES. There are tests that can determine the silver content of coins.

AL. I'm sure your local grocer will want to test every coin that he receives.

CHARLES. At least countries would be able to use gold to transfer large payments between nations to pay off national debts. Large corporations could also use it to buy large shipments of raw materials or finished products.

AL. Under those circumstances I don't believe you will be holding much gold for very long Charles. It sounds to me that the government or large corporations are going to need that gold of yours. Maybe they'll write you an IOU when they take it.

AMY. I'd rather have a few friends I could count on then your pile of gold Charles.

PRISCILLA. That gold you think will make you a survivor is as dead as your soul.

AL. How much income is this gold generating that you're holding?

CHARLES. (*A bit sheepishly*). None., But I'll make my profit when the value of the gold and silver I'm holding begins to rise again.

AL. How much has the price increased over the past year?

CHARLES. It has dropped a little bit.

AL. How much do you have to pay to store it?

CHARLES. Not much. I have it all in safe deposit boxes. I probably pay no more than $1200 per year in safe deposit box rent.

AL. This sounds like a bad investment to me. You're slowly losing money now, and if a catastrophic economic collapse occurs, I doubt you will be much better off than anyone else. You claim to be pessimistic about the economy, but the only way your bet will pay off is if the economy starts to expand so swiftly that consumer demand begins to inflate commodity prices.

PRISCILLA. It serves him right. Following false gods will always lead to confusion and error.

FATHER. By following what you consider to be objective reason, you've landed in a pretty unreasonable position.

CHARLES. At least I'm not following some corrupt, lying politician who will lead us into nothing but trouble, or some fabricated god that will not aide our economic survival in any way. My advice: ban all corrupt politicians and imaginary gods from meddling in the economy. (*He folds his arms.*).

FATHER. Your advice makes little logical sense today, here in this room. Do you think that Al can actually follow your advice?

PRISCILLA. Al created the unholy mess we are in and shouldn't be allowed in the discussion at all.

CHARLES. That's fine by me.

FATHER. We might solve our economic problems if we work as a team, and the team should unearth as many points of view as possible. If we don't we might overlook some of our options. I believe that cutting Al out of the discussion will do just this. Also cutting out the person who can implement our ideas may be a mistake, no mater what we see as his shortcomings.

(*Priscilla and Charles both frown.*)

AL. (*Al swallows hard and looks around the room, then regains his composure*). You also need a leader who can combine your ideas into something you all will support. Right now I don't see anyone else here who can take my place. You can't possibly believe that this group would ever choose you as its leader Charles? Or you Priscilla?

CHARLES. Why not? I'm the only one here who knows how to locate the truth through logic and reason, and unlike you, Al, I place a high value on the truth I discover.

FATHER. Logic and reason are just as much methods for making the truth as for finding it. At least Al knows that he's making his truths. You, on the other hand, can't see that you are too.

CHARLES. I don't make up the facts of existence; they lie before me hidden under a cloak of ignorance waiting for me to uncover them. By its very definition truth cannot be made. It exists beyond the works of man. If man can create it, then it's not truth. It's a fabrication.

PRISCILLA. I agree. I should lead the group. God is the ultimate truth, and I'm the only one here who understands and accepts that truth. We don't make god. Instead God made us.

FATHER. Despite your so-called "faultless" methods of locating the truth, neither of you possess any more certainty where the future will lead us than Amy does. (*He turns to Amy*). Who do you think has the best chance of finding solutions for our economic problems?

AMY. I certainly don't want to lead this group. I either feel something is true or I don't, and I change my mind a lot. This seems to upset a lot of other people. (*She glances over at Priscilla.*) The only things I can know for certain are what I feel, and while I might change my mind... I feel you should lead us

(*Al smiles and stands a little straighter*).

WHY CAN'T WE
BE FRIENDS?

AL. (*Straightens his tie and smiles broadly*). Thank you Amy. If you allow me to lead you, we will blaze a new path to economic safety through the... Um... Internet.

AMY. (*Looking at Al with the beginnings of admiration*). You already have a plan, don't you? (*Al nods*). It involves the Internet doesn't it? (*Al nods again*). You will need to put more resources into education if you're going to staff this new Internet economy with skilled people who can perform these jobs. (*Unaware that Al has stopped nodding, Amy begins to get excited*). You're planning on putting money back into all the education budgets aren't you?

AL. Er yes,.. Probably... I will though we will need to find new ways to make our educational systems more cost effective and efficient. We won't be able to afford to use our present methods of education given our current level of resources. I'm going to need your help Amy in coming up with new ideas that will allow us to school millions of people quickly. Do you think you can do that for me?

AMY. I'd rather you just spent more money so I could have my job back, but I will help you if I can.

PRISCILLA. I can't believe you think Al will do anything to save you Amy. Why do you believe anything that comes out of his mouth?

AMY. I believe him, because he is the only person here who is trying to fix the economy and avoid the end of days, economic or otherwise, that you and Charles so firmly expect. I'm sorry Daddy, but I haven't heard any solutions from you either, just uncertainty about what they might be.

FATHER. (*Smiles and nods his head in the affirmative*).

PRISCILLA. I'm willing to help you Amy, if you are willing to help your-self. (*Amy looks at her blankly*). You must learn to improve your character if you want to survive tough times with happiness

FATHER. (*Considering Priscilla's last statement*). Charles, you've focused too much on what you feel to be objectively measurable causes of our economic problems. I believe there are a number of other causes for our problems that it is impossible for you to view objectively much less mea-sure accurately; causes that you would consider to be purely emotional and insubstantial, though still very real and relevant to our economic problems. We should consider the emotional roots that give rise to our economic problems, and possibly look for some emotional solutions.

AL. (*Smiles*). Now you're talking my language Pops.

CHARLES. No emotion ever solved a real problem.

AMY. Emotions just confuse Charles. He doesn't think they should exist because his reason and logic can't manage them.

AL. And yet he is just as vulnerable to the influence of emotion as the rest of us.

FATHER. (*Nods*). Charles, your desire to separate yourself from other people and retreat to some hypothetical island of stability and "brightness" is as much an emotional response as anything your brother or sisters have expressed. Al will have to deal with these feelings of yours and of people like you if he is to fix our economy even temporarily. These feelings may have caused you to lose sight of the fact that we are all intimately involved in the same economy. Separation is impossible. We share common problems, and your attitude of every man for himself just makes these problems more likely to worsen. Such an attitude causes us to become blind to the positive efforts of all the other people operating within our economy. You end up failing to appreciate how their cooperation has already made your economic life better. Yes, competition and individual effort can invigorate an economy and push it to expand, but it can also tear an economy apart, if left unchecked, or becomes an economy's only ingredient. Amy's instinctive feeling that friendship serves a necessary role in every economy is as valid as your understanding that some competition is also necessary and probably inevitable. (Amy beams). Any recipe for a cake of economic health should include both of these ingredients, along with the acceptance that the inhuman and mysterious "invisible hand of god" will also fall into the mix somehow and possibly affect the resulting outcome in an unpredictable manner. Sometimes we will follow the recipe faithfully, but the cake will still fall flat. We have to be ready to deal with that eventuality as a group.

AMY. Friendship isn't enough? Won't any economy always get better if we all help each other out?

AL. That's a big "if". As much as I'd like to see it happen, it's pretty unlikely. Though I do see your point, I have to do more to get you three and all the rest of my constituents to work together.

CHARLES. Even if by some stretch of the imagination you could convince us to help each other at a cost to ourselves, this cooperation still wouldn't ensure success.

PRISCILLA. Your economy of only winners and losers also won't ensure success Charles.

AL. I used to think that capitalism required there be only Charles' winners and losers, now I see that we're all starting to lose under such a mind set. Yes, up until recently capitalism has improved the well being of the majority of citizens, but recently it has been creating a lot more losers than winners. This sad situation should give us all cause for hope, (*Everyone looks at Al with puzzlement*). If we now live in an economy where all can lose, possibly we can finally work together to modify it so that all can win.

PRISCILLA. We didn't all lose during the economic downturn. The wealthy capitalists who got us into that mess continued to do well because they were bailed out by people like you who I'm sure also made out all right.

CHARLES. He did. The money he pulled out of my business benefited only him and not me. The financial crisis clearly produced winners as well as losers, and any solution you develop will do the same. We can't all win.

AL. Most of the people and institutions the government bailed out didn't win; they just survived. There might have been a few people who guessed right and made a bundle from the collapse, but most people didn't. I certainly don't consider myself one of the winners, and I sincerely want to reformulate the economy so that a similar crisis never happens again. Stop crying, Charles, you knew that stem cell research business of yours was already a lost cause. I notice that you sold the business not long after I got out, probably to someone who didn't understand what he was buying.

You know as well as I do, that I didn't quite break even when I sold out my shares of the business.

CHARLES. You should have lost a lot more money for abandoning me like you did, and like most of the my other investors eventually did.

PRISCILLA. I can't feel sorry for either of you or for any of your idle investor friends. You were all gambling against each other. I doubt any of you tried to see anything beyond making a quick profit. You are going to have to take a long term view that reaches well beyond making a simple profit for yourselves if you are to successfully remedy our ailing economy.

AMY. (*Puzzled.*) Al, I thought you didn't like Charles. You've made just as much fun of him as I have over the years. How could you ever become his partner?

AL. (*Looks a little shamefaced and shrugs his shoulders*). We decided to help each other out. I like helping people out. You know that.

AMY. (*Thinks for a second*). That I understand. That's how my friends and I deal with our economic problems, though I use something else for money! (Everyone looks at her with raised eyebrows). I don't need cash, or stocks or bonds, or even paid employment to sustain myself. My friends and I trade various things we need, and do favors for each other.

PRISCILLA. I'll bet.

AMY. For example, a couple of times a week my friends and I meet at someone's house where we pool our food and make a potluck dinner.

FATHER. That sounds like a practice the early Christians, Priscilla, undertook during their darkest days. Surely this is a practice that you support.

PRISCILLA. It's not at all Christian. I hear that after dinner they smoke marijuana and party into the early morning hours.

AMY. That's not true Priscilla! Who in the world is telling you these stories?

PRISCILLA. (*Folds her arms and says nothing*).

AMY. I also sometimes watch my friend's children while she's on a job interview. She's a single mom and has no one else to watch her kids.

PRISCILLA. Why doesn't she have a husband? Do you watch her children when she's out dating other men?

AMY. I help her whenever I can.

CHARLES. I hope she didn't decide to leave her husband during the economic downturn. That would have been extremely impractical

AMY. Mary has cut my hair and I paid her with a loaf of bread I made. Joe repaired Ralph's car and Ralph repaired Joe's roof in return. It all works out really well. Why just yesterday my friend Paul came over to fix my gas stove and hot water heater.

PRISCILLA. And what did he get in return?

AMY. I baked him a cake.

FATHER. You seem to disapprove, Priscilla. Why?

PRISCILLA. Amy knows why. (*Amy avoids her glance*).

FATHER. This kind of barter of goods and services is more likely to form the basis of any working economy that would operate after the economic collapse that Charles predicts. Barter combines practicality with a tradition that people already know and are willing to fall back on. Sometimes it works quite well.

AL. I can't tell my constituents that the answer to their economic problems should be a barter economy. I wouldn't even vote for myself under such a platform. People may be willing to barter if they have to, but no one really wants to go through the trouble of doing it. A cash economy makes life a lot easier and comfortable for everybody.

AMY. It's not so difficult.

CHARLES. (*Laughing*) Maybe a barter economy isn't so bad. I like the fact that you couldn't collect income taxes on bartered transactions. Though I doubt that Al would approve of that type of economic stimulus. (*Smirks sarcastically*).

PRISCILLA. Joseph and Mary paid their taxes with grain, though if you lived then Charles I'm sure you would have found another way to avoid paying anything.

AL. You still need some sort of money and profit for your barter economy to work, Amy. Someone needed money for the materials to fix your friends' car and roof.

FATHER. Yes, all barter economies need some form of agreed upon currency to lubricate all but the most basic transactions.

Al Besides that, how do people determine and compare the value of each good or service bartered?

AMY. We just know.

AL. How do you know you've gotten a fair deal when you replace a roof in return for having your car fixed? How do you know these services are of equal value? Perhaps one friend is taking advantage of the other, and his service is worth a lot less than the one he receives. Do you keep track of the time it takes to perform the service, the skills required by the services, or the value of the parts needed to perform the service? A competitive market that uses money as a marker can make all these decisions quite quickly and efficiently.

AMY. We really don't care if the goods and services we trade are exactly of the same value. If it feels right we make the trade. If I have a backed up toilet that is spilling waste onto my bathroom floor, I might throw in an extra loaf of bread to have it fixed to show my appreciation for quick assistance. Barter requires no accounting, and no profit and loss statements. We exchange what we have to exchange without expecting to make a profit, or even to break even.

CHARLES. If you don't make a profit, why do it? If you make a lot of profitless trades you will soon have nothing left to trade. Where will you be then?

AMY. We'll be happy. We do it partly because we like helping each other out. You can't put a price on that feeling.

FATHER. I admire the little economic system you've built amongst your friends, Amy.

It seems to be working for you, and Al might be able to integrate some idea of mutual assistance into any of his broader economic plans. It might be possible to somehow combine mutual cooperation with mutual competition in a hybrid economic system, but I wonder how well your barter economy works between your group and outsiders who are not your friends.

AMY. (*Looks at her feet*). So far, not so well. They don't trust us. They want money, and usually as much as they can get.

CHARLES. They make rational decisions, unlike you and your friends.

AMY. We've tried to expand our group, but we always run up against people who don't want to be our friends. Some contend they don't even want to know us. They just want our money. If we could all trust each other and be friends, I think most of our economic problems would disappear.

FATHER. Maybe they wouldn't. You need to consider this possibility.

CHARLES. The value of the goods and services your economy produces is not only vague and subjective but also miniscule. It can never support the millions of people that make up modern economies.

AL. Amy, my experience in politics has taught me that you'll never get everyone to treat each other as friends. Hell, the four of us, can't even be friends. People will always look out for themselves and their friends first and disagree about the value of what others have to offer.

PRISCILLA. Some people can't help but take advantage of each other. That is the fallen nature of man.

FATHER. Most people don't instinctively want to exploit each other. They learn to do that.

AL. Yes, people come to expect that others will try to take advantage of them, and as a result, find it easier to take advantage of others in turn. Trust and the reason to trust usually fade as any group grows larger and larger. This causes individual competition to expand and creates immense problems. As much as I agree with Charles' notion that all economies must revolve around competition for limited resources, I can see where competition by itself often creates more problems than it solves, I think that any economic solution I develop must promote both competition and cooperation amongst its participants.

CHARLES. I will accept this insight Al, because competition and cooperation are both facts that can be observed, measured and controlled. I agree that they should be part of any successful economic mix. What I object to is this importance father puts on perception as an essential ingredient in all economic systems. Perceptions are fluid and at times complete illusions. An economic system must be built on substance, on hard facts: the amount of money in circulation, existing interest rates, profit and loss, and supply and demand. All economies are created and maintained out of facts such as these and not out of human perceptions and "feelings".

AL. Still, I wish more of my constituents possessed the feelings Amy and her friends have for each other. They don't rely on some outside authority to bail them out, nor do they compete with each other in a cutthroat manner for whatever resources are available. It would certainly help me in my efforts to fix the economy.

PRISCILLA. Why should we make your job easier? You and your kind caused this problem, not us. We've been punished for your greed and incompetence.

AL. Everyone had a hand in it, even you.

PRISCILLA. I've never supported any of your hair brained government programs, nor your blind faith in capitalism, and when the recession hit I actually helped the people who needed it when I created a food pantry to feed my flock. You on the other hand, focused only on helping capitalists like Charles find the shirts they had lost, or thrown away foolishly.

AL. What have you done for Amy and her friends?

PRISCILLA. I know who they are, and they are all sinners, unworthy of my or God's help. I help only those who follow Jesus dictum of 'go forth and sin no more".

AMY. Whom exactly do you give your food out to then? I've heard you claim that we're all sinners, except for yourself, of course.

PRISCILLA. (*Blushing a bit while looking over at Amy*). Some sin more carelessly than others.

FATHER. So you don't believe in sharing the food you've gathered with everyone?

PRISCILLA. We should share only with the people who deserve a share. Some do not. These are the unrepentant ones who God will deny entry into the Kingdom of God.

AMY. How do you know who are the few people good enough to receive your charity?

AL. (*Snickers*). Perhaps the same ones who will live on Charles islands of enlightenment.

PRISCILLA. They live in a morally upright manner. They are the people who strive to maintain a good character in the face of temptation. They possess moral and ethical discipline and sincerely search for work if they do not have it, and hold onto that job no matter how onerous it may become.

AL. If you only give food to people who already have a job you are not helping those most in need. That's not what I would do. Government poverty programs don't always work as well as planned, but at least we try to get aide out to the people who need it most.

PRISCILLA. To help the indolent is to reward them. Why do you want to encourage such behavior? If you withdrew all the benefits that Amy, her friends, and people like them currently receive, they would see that their only option would be to get off their couches and start working. If you stopped helping them, they, with god's inspiration, would learn to help themselves.

AL. Without the benefits government provided, they would help themselves all right Priscilla, though I doubt your god would like how they go about doing it.

CHARLES. You would just need to spend a few more dollars on law enforcement Al, and you've solved that problem. While I don't believe that Priscilla's god is going to help anyone find employment, I do agree with her in that we should not pay people to be unemployed. Doing so increases my taxes, and removes capital from my pocket that I may need for future investments. You are forcing me to give my money to people who offer me no labor in return. There is no reason for me to give them anything.

AMY. That's cold and heartless Charles.

FATHER. Since you have the ability to help them, you have an obligation to help.

CHARLES. Our most important obligation is to ourselves and our own survival Life offers up only one prime directive and that is to survive. If our survival is predicated on someone else not surviving, so be it.

FATHER. You want to live in a society based on the law of the jungle? Beware Charles; you may not find such a society conducive to your own survival (*Al, Amy, and Priscilla all glare steadily at Charles*).

CHARLES. All right, maybe the "law of the jungle" isn't what I want, but my economic success will always result from a society where others don't benefit from it as much as I do. Sorry, that's the way it is.

AL. (*Shakes his head sadly*). Amy, I fear that your brother and sister are not willing to share as much as you do. They won't be baking any cakes for you any time soon.

CHARLES. Don't act like you are better than me You want to succeed at your opponent's expense, or do you want to give him your Senate seat? If you lose perhaps you will bake a cake for your opponent? You want to end up better off than everyone else as much as Priscilla and I do.

PRISCILLA. I don't want to end up better off than others like you do Charles. I'm already better off because of my love and understanding of God.

AL. I want to be elected, yes, but I know that can happen only if I find a way to improve the lives of almost everybody else. I know that an attitude of every man for himself, in your case Charles, and of helping only those you deem to be deserving Priscilla, will result in everyone, the good, the bad and the ugly facing insurmountable difficulties. No one will succeed, and the only survivors will be those selected not by your law of the fittest Charles, but by blind chance. The economic environment will become so grim that the few so-called survivors will in no way consider themselves successes, and survival will feel like a curse.

REGULATE OR DIE?

AMY. If not enough people will help each other out of the goodness of their hearts is there any other way that people can be made to share?

FATHER. Yes, Al and his colleagues can regulate the economy and tax the economy's winners to fund goods and services for people like you who need them.

CHARLES. (*Shakes his head*). Sure, tax the only productive people you have. We'll just walk away, and move our businesses and capital to another country. When that happens you'll have no economy at all.

AMY. My friends and I will still share what we've got no matter where you move.

AL. Eventually, you will face the same tax and regulatory obligations in your new location. If governments **don't** tax and regulate businesses so that the wealth they create, as a team, is spread out more evenly across their economy, social unrest will destroy both.

CHARLES. It might take years before those obligations, or on the other hand, that kind of social upheaval will occur. In the meantime I could make a tidy profit.

FATHER. I doubt there would be anything tidy about it. Trade barriers to counter the economic inequities between countries that you want to exploit would reduce your export sales, and if you don't transfer enough wealth to your new workers for them to buy much of whatever you're selling your domestic market will also shrink. How do you plan to make a profit under those conditions? You share common interests with your workers and with the public at large whether you like it or not.

CHARLES. Amy's turned you both into Socialists. Competition always trumps common interests, and nobody wins if nobody loses. You've completely given up on capitalism, Al, haven't you?

AL. No, not at all. Capitalism will continue to be the horse that pulls the cart of the economy. I just plan to put all of us in that cart and take the reins of regulation to encourage the horse to carry us forward so that we can proceed as a group to where we all want to go. Your form of capitalism isn't the only one. We Capitalists can and do have all sorts of conflicting beliefs.

CHARLES. What if I disagree with you about where you want to take the economy? What if I want the cart to carry us to my house instead of Priscilla's? When government reins in capitalism in any manner you remove some of its power to motivate people to use it because it now won't take them where they really want to go. If they don't like the government's destination they won't invest, innovate and take the risks necessary for long-term economic growth.

AL. Charles, I don't particularly like regulation or taxes either. I admit they both undermine capitalism's two main benefits: its efficiency and potential for growth, but people like you who refuse to share your success and deal honorably with those who lose out under capitalist systems leave me no other alternative.

AMY. I don't understand. How can fairness and sharing possibly hurt an economy, or be bad in any way?

AL. When you raise taxes, you reduce the amount of available capital that business owners can invest back into their businesses. This means they have less money to pay their employees, purchase efficiency-improving machines, or purchase all the raw materials they need to build the best products. This limits production. Also, if taxes become too high the potential rewards from the business will not be sufficient to justify the owner's risk of losing his capital in a bad investment.

AMY. Bad investment? What does that mean?

PRISCILLA. The people hired were lazy and sloppy.

CHARLES. Skilled workers couldn't be hired as cheaply as planned or the machinery purchased to replace these workers didn't work as well as expected.

AL. Investors lose money in a bad investment Amy. They may lose it for any number of reasons such as buyers not finding the product as useful or attractive as the investor originally thought they would, (*He peers over at Charles*). When such a loss occurs, the business owner has less, and sometimes no more capital to invest further. When no new investments pour into an economy, the economy can create no new wealth to be shared with its participants.

FATHER. True, capitalism creates new wealth only when the capitalist's investment pays off. If it fails to do so, wealth may simply evaporate. You need to keep in mind, however, that taxes and regulation do not always determine whether an investment will succeed or fail. Most of the time other factors determine this. A lot of wealth was destroyed in the recent economic crash, not because taxes were too high, and especially not because regulation was too strict, but because the relationship between the risk and reward of various investments was not understood properly. The risks were greater than what investors thought they were. Investors poured money into leveraged debt and other, more arcane investment vehicles because they didn't perceive the real risks involved. Perhaps they would have been more careful about where they invested their money if the taxes on potential profits had been higher and their expected profits lower. Perhaps better and more comprehensive government regulations would have prevented them from making such risky investments at all.

CHARLES. Investors often perceive the risks of an investment quite correctly father; and when you tax their potential profits too much, they will cut back on all investments risky or otherwise. I'm certain that you wouldn't want to promote such a deleterious outcome, now would you?

AMY. Why doesn't the government raise and lower taxes as investors become more or less enthusiastic, Al? Raise taxes when the economy and people's greed heats up and investors start moving their money into riskier investments, and lower taxes when the economy struggles and they become afraid to invest in much of anything?

FATHER. The problem with this idea is that both investors and the government must base their respective decisions on "perception", and perceptions are often incorrect. No one, no government and no investor, can ever be certain that their perception of the relationship between the risk and return in a specific investment reflects reality. Despite all the data gathered, no one can be absolutely certain how healthy an economy as a whole has become or is becoming. Finally, no one can be absolutely certain that they understand what causes any identified economic problem, what its solution should be, or when to implement it.

AL. Generally speaking, Amy, governments often do lower taxes and the cost of borrowing when the business climate is gloomy, and raise them when it brightens up.

AMY. It doesn't feel like it's working right now.

AL. No, we can't implement that remedy the way we want right now. People are afraid to spend and invest enough to really get the economy rolling, but I'm told that we can't lower taxes, because the government needs more tax revenue to provide you with the financial support and health care you need. Schools need more funds to operate. Businesses need more and safer roads and bridges to move their products more efficiently. All this costs money. I'm told we should both raise and lower taxes. I don't know which way to turn.

FATHER. Rather than raise taxes you could lower interest rates or run a budget deficit to fund the services the public needs while finding other incentives to encourage business people to invest their capital into new enterprises.

PRISCILLA. Be careful. Remember the Biblical admonition: Neither a borrower nor lender be.

CHARLES. There are no other incentives to encourage business investment other than lowering taxes and increasing the amount of potential profit. Raising the deficit only means that you will have to raise our taxes sometime in the future to pay off this debt. We business people know that will happen and factor it into our business plans. It raises the risk that we will not profit from our future investments.

FATHER. You don't really have a clear idea of the dimensions of that risk. It's merely a subjective perception. This perception of the amount of future risk can be changed by building confidence and optimism among the participants of the economy. You keep forgetting that economic reality, like all reality is partly constructed by the human imagination. If you can convince people to see that the economy can get better, it is likely that it will. Talented leaders can also change the perception of what constitutes an appropriate and successful profit. Lately corporate executives expect huge paychecks because their peers are getting them. For them, a comfortable income forty years ago represents a pittance today and hardly worth the effort of operating a business. Investors expect double-digit returns on their investments when a return of 4% or 5% was acceptable in the past. People were satisfied with much smaller rewards. Investors gradually scraped out modest profits from their investments and considered themselves a success. Perhaps Al, you and other leaders allowed the definition of economic success to become unrealistic before the recent economic swoon. I believe that real estate had increased in value by more than 100% during the ten years preceding the crash. People expected that this was the new normal and could continue forever, when a more realistic expectation should have been much lower.

CHARLES. I finally agree with you about something, father. There is no reason that a house should increase in value beyond the general rate of inflation unless the population increases by the same percentage. In fact, if the population doesn't increase, the value of a real estate might reasonably decrease somewhat as properties age and begin to wear out. The reasonable increase in the price of a house should be the inflation rate adjusted by any increase in the local population.

FATHER. I don't know how you can be so certain. You again place too much faith in data and false objectivity. The number of people who need a house is not simply a matter of the increase in population. As people become wealthier, they desire larger houses, and vacation homes. Some of those who previously wanted a house but could not afford to buy one now can.

AL. I'm confused, Father. What do you want me to do now? Raise everyone's expectations of increased wealth and general economic growth so they will possess the confidence to go forth and spend and invest more or lower them so that people won't become disappointed later on when reality doesn't meet such optimistic expectations.

FATHER. I don't know. I'm not the master of split second timing that you claim to be. Follow your instincts and common sense after reviewing Charles "objective" economic data. Always remember, there is a time to spend, a time to lower taxes, a time to lower interest rates, and a time to tighten budgets, raise taxes, and increase interest rates. Unlike what the various partisan economists claim, none of these moves are inherently good or bad. What matters is when and how you perform each. Timing is everything. Don't let yourself fall into the clutches of any economic orthodoxy that prevents you from taking any useful action.

AL. (*Smiles knowingly*). I can do that!

FATHER. Like an ice climber scaling a sheer wall you must carefully observe the uncertain economy and develop a feeling for it before you move on. You develop this intuitive "feel" by talking to your constituents, determining which of their many problems seems most critical to their wealth and happiness, and comparing your impressions against the economic data provided by economists who do not have an important stake in their recommendations, if you can find one.

CHARLES. (*Looks angrily at his father*). You recommend he follow some vague, subjective phantasm and ignore all the verifiable data that has allowed economists to accurately predict economic policy in the past? That is madness, and look at what kind of poor decision makers will be taking such advice! (*He points to Amy*)

FATHER. I don't want him to ignore economic data at all. In fact, he should always keep one eye on the numbers. I recommend, however, that he not focus exclusively on them. I don't believe that your so-called "objective" economic data describe or predict the health of the economy as well as you seem to think, and any single-minded approach in solving a difficult problem will usually lead one astray. As Ralph Waldo Emerson once stated, "The glance reveals what the gaze obscures". Al needs to rely on more than data to manage the unpredictability of our large and complex economy.

CHARLES. His "intuition" had better not lead him to raise taxes or interest rates. If he does, he will stifle what little economic growth that now exists. That's a proven fact.

FATHER. It's a common perception.

CHARLES. Al, I know you. You're as much of a Capitalist as me. You want to be a winner. You always do. Do you really want to water down the economic system that has made this country, and you and me great? Don't get all emotional and irrational on me like our sisters do, or question everything like Father.

AL. It has worked well in the past, and I haven't given up on it, but I'm willing to change my mind as the economy heads in a new direction. I've never come across any two economic situations or solutions that were exactly alike, and capitalism must also exist in many different flavors. Rather than play the same song over and over again, a successful musician learns many tunes to entertain the public. I'm elected to make choices, and not to just follow the dictates of some economic religion. If I don't believe there are any new choices to be made, then I'm not doing the job the public elected me to do. (*He smiles at both Priscilla and Amy. Amy smiles back. Priscilla becomes thoughtful*).

CHARLES. Flitting from one choice to another will never bring you success; it will just confuse the public and make it harder for businessmen like me to make plans for future investments.

AL. Sticking with a broken method won't bring us success either.

FATHER. (*Nods*).

AL. Don't worry Charles, I'm not going to recommend we raise taxes right away. That, ah, doesn't seem wise at the moment. Instead, I'll support any efforts the government makes to borrow or print more money to fund the increase in government services I now see are needed. I am going to ask my brothers and sisters in Congress to immediately take a firmer hand in regulating businesses. Like taxation, the amount of regulation should vary according to the current market conditions. Now, in light of the recent economic meltdown caused partly by a lack of enforced rules, it seems like a fine moment to increase it.

PRISCILLA. You've finally come to your senses. You are wrong to suppose, however, that there will ever be a good time to reduce regulation. Our Government must always apply strict controls upon businesses and the economy because people, people like you Charles, will always be greedy and try to prey upon their fellow man. Human nature will never change, and regulation needs to be constant and vigorous no matter how healthy the economy may become.

AL. Regulation is a bit like medicine. You need to take it to cure a sick situation, but applying too much medicine to a healthy patient can have dangerous side effects, and eventually make the patient sicker. Human nature may not change much Priscilla, but it's not all bad. Sometimes you have to sit back and allow the best parts to bloom without yanking it out with the weeds. I want to produce a beautiful garden rather than punish an occasional errant weed.

PRISCILLA. If you ask me, the weeds have taken over your garden. This economic crash was created by the untrammeled greed of individual investors trying to make a quick buck with other people's money. They didn't want to build or make anything. They wanted only to initiate trades that moved money from other people's pockets to their own as quickly as possible.

AMY. Business people have hurt us in other ways too. They have ruined the air we breathe and the water we drink. They ruin our health. They are even destroying the climate. Your so-called garden is dying, and you've done nothing about it.

AL. I have done much.....

PRISCILLA. Capitalists don't care who they hurt, Amy. You say you believe in regulating businesses, but you've done next to nothing. Now, after they have done their worst, you plan to add a little regulation. Whatever you're planning to do, it won't be enough. These criminals need to be bound in the chains of justice and forced to repent their sins. You must never allow them to hurt the rest of us again.

AL. That's a pretty tall order. I can't eliminate greed only regulate it.

PRISCILLA. You've regulated nothing. Instead, you've accepted greed as the normal state of affairs under the golden spires of your cathedral of capitalism.

CHARLES. If we're so evil, Priscilla, then why doesn't your god just smite us like he did in your Bible? He's the ultimate regulator, right?

PRISCILLA. Perhaps he will. Your time is running out, Charles.

FATHER. Perhaps we need regulation a little less radical than throwing all capitalists into regulatory chains. I think we need rules that will nudge investors and managers away from short-term goals and measures of success to more long term ones. Too many people currently chase quick profits. They want a big, immediate payoff. It is this attitude that supports program trading of stocks and bonds, trading in derivatives, trading on inside information, corporate balance sheet manipulation, tax evasion, government corruption, and outright fraud.

PRISCILLA. Just making something illegal that gives violators a little slap on the wrist will never stop people. This is indeed a corrupt and fallen world filled with nothing but cruelty, injustice, and greed. Humanity will never flourish until Al performs his job with the Wisdom of Solomon and the resolve of Joshua or until God destroys this world and all of the selfish competition that lies within it. God will create a new world devoid of shameless exploitation where the lion will lie down with the lamb if Al isn't up to the task.

FATHER. Regulation may not end greed, selfishness, and cruelty, but it might harness these unfortunate human characteristics to the point where they can be managed. Maybe if we regulate capitalism better, we can create something both practical and beneficial out of our baser motives.

AL. (*Quick to pick up on his father's idea*). Yes, exactly! Maybe if we bridle and saddle these darker aspects of ourselves, they can take us somewhere we all want to go. (*Amy nods expectantly*). Maybe if we develop regulations that limit the profitability of speculative investments like derivatives, more productive long-term investments will result. (Amy sighs and begins to lose interest).

AL. What else would you have me do, Amy? What would you like me to do first? What do you want?

CHARLES. (*Snorts*). Some change that is. You really have no plan. You do just do whatever the unthinking masses want.

AMY. Rather than make up a bunch of new rules, could you help my students by giving some of your own money to the school so they can buy new textbooks this year?

CHARLES. (*Rolls his eyes*). A drop in the bucket. It won't change the economy one whit.

AMY. and encourage your fellow legislators and friends to do the same to their local schools?

PRISCILLA. How will the donors know the schools really need these textbooks? How will they know whose pockets the book money will end up in? You need some rules to keep everyone honest.

CHARLES. More importantly, how will the donors know that their donations really pay for needed textbooks, and not for some unworthy projects like staff salary increases?

AMY. They could meet and get to know my school's teachers and administrators. As a matter of fact, you, Charles, should meet them. You might find them more than worthy of their paychecks. It doesn't help much to just write a check and walk away. The donors and school staff need to get to know each other if our schools are ever going to get back on their feet again. We need to get back to the kind of relationships we had when most of us lived in small towns. You know, where everyone knew everyone else. Back then, we knew to give food rather than money to the town drunk. We knew quiet ways to get help to people who were too proud to ask for it. We knew when they no longer needed help as well.

PRISCILLA. You want a society where everyone knows everybody else's business. I would think you wouldn't like that.

AMY. Everybody already seems to know my business. Notoriety spreads fast. It's deep-seated goodness that remains hidden. Small towns have their drawbacks, but it's a massive improvement over Charles' heartless jungle or your vengeful Kingdom of God.

AL. (*Manages a weak smile toward Amy*). Most of my constituents don't live in small towns. They live in cities or suburbs. These people don't have the time or opportunity to get to know one another, much less help each other.

AMY. They should make time and seek opportunities.

AL. I don't see how your idea will work, but I will make a donation to your school, and encourage my friends to do the same. I will even visit it to see how the books are being used, (*He glances up at Charles*), and meet your former students.

PRISCILLA. Since you're making promises, how about promising that when you talk to these well-fixed friends of yours, you convince them that they are no better than anyone else. Tell them that they are sinners, not winners.

AL. I'll leave that up to you, Priscilla. I will let everyone I meet know that all of us, the rich and the poor, the winners and the losers, the successes, and the failures are all splashing around together in the same economic mess. Some may be only up to their ankles in this mess, (*He looks sternly at Charles*), while others will soon be totally underwater. To clean up the mess we're in, we must engage in some kind of teamwork and seek broader economic goals than individual profits. Some aspect of Amy's economy of sharing has to be incorporated into capitalism. Yes, I can see in what direction I need to steer our economy, and character does play a big part in any solution, Priscilla. I can see strengths in my soul that maybe you cannot. I honestly believe that only I have the talents and temperament to fix the economy. Father, I didn't have it before, but I now see that I possess the confidence to fix everything! I lost a sense of confidence in myself as advisors, and the public buffeted me back and forth across various points of view that I didn't actually believe. I've now found what I really believe, and that is that I can save us all.

FATHER. I'm glad to hear that, but it's going to take more than just self-confidence to solve your problems. Specifically, what regulations do you want to implement?

AL. (*Pauses for a moment.*)

Well. I'm open to ideas. (*Al looks around the room. Amy looks puzzled. Charles sits closed mouth with his arms folded across his chest. Priscilla takes out her Bible and begins to search its pages*).

FATHER. For example, how about giving corporations a small tax break if they base the size of bonuses they give to their managers on the average profits for a five-year period instead of only for the previous year as they do now? Instead of giving a manager a 20% bonus for one year's performance, you could give him a 20% bonus based on the past five year's profits. Next year's bonus would be calculated on the previous five years, and so on.

CHARLES. That means no manager would receive a bonus for the first four years he works. That's a pretty shabby incentive for staff you want to work sixty-hour workweeks.

AL. (*Grateful that his father has come up with an idea*). Sounds good to me. It might take him five years to become really productive. He probably wouldn't deserve a bonus for the first four years he works for the company. Other people's efforts would have more effect on the company's bottom line during that time.

CHARLES. The really talented people start producing and innovating the first day on the job. Those who don't immediately increase profits are quickly terminated. Anyway, this bonus would still provide an incentive for managers to cook the books and show a profit during the years when there was none.

FATHER. It would be much harder to manipulate the profit and loss figures for five years than for one. Also, the bonus could be structured so that the manager would continue to receive a reward for the next four years after he leaves the firm on the condition that the profits reported for the years the manager was involved hold up under audit scrutiny. If the profit the manager reported for the years in question proves to be bogus, the manager would have to pay back any bonus he had already received for the period in question.

CHARLES. If it were me, and I knew I had cooked the books, I would just spend my bonus as quickly as possible and declare bankruptcy when I was caught.

PRISCILLA. What vermin you capitalists are.

CHARLES. (*Charles looks shocked. Then he pulls himself together to put on a brazen face*). Vermin. That's no insult. Cockroaches, rats, and others you might characterize as vermin are all tremendous survivors. They should be admired because survival is what life is all about.

PRISCILLA. None of this ugliness and injustice you call capitalism deserves to survive. It can't be regulated. Cockroaches can be stamped out only by the total destruction of this corrupt, unredeemable world.

CHARLES. The justice and fairness that you think so important don't exist anywhere. They are fantasies created by your fevered imagination. They possess no substance at all, and neither does this kingdom of god where you think they reside.

PRISCILLA. As human beings, we are unique among all of God's creatures in that we have the ability, indeed the right, to improve our empty, heartless, natural world by eliminating its greed and cruelty. I would start out by eliminating you!

AL. Something always survives, and it's not always the vermin, Charles, and it's certainly not always the righteous Priscilla. It's my job to see that as many people as possible survive and even thrive. Neither of you seems to have any interest in doing the same thing. It seems I serve a purpose than either of you after all. (*He smiles*).

CHARLES. I can't imagine what that would be.

AL. For one thing, I protect you from each other.

PRISCILLA. We wouldn't need your "protection" if people showed evidence of godliness and good character. I suggest that if you want to find the true cause of our economic apocalypse, we should investigate the honesty and righteousness of the economy's so-called movers and shakers rather than Charles' deceitful economic facts and so-called natural laws. You all need to take a look at yourselves before you can solve anyone else's problems.

The Mote in my Brother's Eye?

FATHER. What do you mean by character?

PRISCILLA. Lack of character is more to the point. Lack of character has caused all of our troubles. The lack of honesty by political leaders like Al, heartless businesspeople like Charles, and weak people like Amy has caused the invisible hand of God to smite the economy and rain economic retribution on us all.

AL. Now, what have I done wrong?

PRISCILLA. You encouraged the greed of capitalism. You allowed businesspeople to take advantage of the working poor. You allowed the unregulated casino of derivative markets to continue unchecked. You knew that the economy was nothing more than a Ponzi scheme and yet did nothing about it. You looked the other way and shirked your responsibility because you took massive campaign contributions from those who would temporarily benefit from these abominations. You and your friends "knew the price of everything and the value of nothing"* (Oscar Wilde).

FATHER. Hmm. She does have a point, Al, though I doubt you were solely responsible for the economic meltdown, by thinking only of yourself and your own needs, you have served as a poor role model for your constituents. Great leaders lead by example.

AMY. You never tried very hard to show us our common interests, and as a result, we've become more and more focused on our own selfish interests. With only you to look up to, we drifted apart. Some of us became totally isolated. (*She looks over at Charles*). We started thinking only about our individual survival because we saw you do the same thing. We stopped feeling for each other. (*Looks at Priscilla*) We became self-important islands rejecting all the rest of humanity that surrounds us. Our economic problems reflect this change in how we see others and ourselves. You led us to this sorry place,

AL. I may not have been the best role model Amy, but you have to believe me, I never intended to lead you to a place where you wouldn't want to take care of each other, and I certainly never intended the economy to put you all in the position you're now in. In fact, my intentions were just the opposite. I wanted the economy to take care of each of you. I led you where I thought each of you wanted to go.

CHARLES. That was a big mistake since we all wanted to go to a different place. (*Priscilla nods in approval*).

AMY. Yet we all ended up in the same economic hard times.

PRISCILLA. That's not true. During the recent financial crisis, most of the money people lost went into the pockets of a few wealthy scoundrels.

AL. (*Looks uncomfortably at his feet*). No, many wealthy people lost money too.

CHARLES. That's right, Al, the government charged usurious interest rates to floundering capitalists and poured the return of these loans into the pockets of idle, good for nothing common people, who added nothing to the economy, and who wasted the money you gave them on non-productive expenditures. (*He glances over at Amy.*)

AMY. Do you really think that any person can be good for nothing? Can't you see that it is good just to be human?

PRISCILLA. Mammon has corrupted his heart. Fear not, Amy, God will cast him down with holy vengeance.

CHARLES. This nut job can say whatever she wants, Al, but you waste any money you give to unproductive people, and you can't afford to waste any more time and money than you already have. If you want to turn this economy around, you'd better be ready to become more hard-headed, practical, and objective than you have been so far.

FATHER. These "unproductive" people, as you call them, spend the money the government has given them on necessities like food, fuel, utilities, and sometimes on other items they need like clothes and furniture. They provide a market for these items. This is hardly a useless function. Without someone to buy goods and services, there is no point in producing them. I'm sure you don't want to persuade Al to eliminate this market.

CHARLES. If all of the world's unproductive people disappeared, yes, our economy and everyone else's would be smaller. I admit that, but these economies would also be much more efficient, and, I believe, a lot fairer. These economies would consist of only productive people, people who could pull their own weight in producing goods and services, and less wasted capital and labor would result. Economies are machines where extra, useless parts get in the way and cause the engine to break down continually.

FATHER. That economy would be so small that it could not produce large amounts of the wealth that you seem to admire so much. I wonder if the hard-working participants of this economy would be very happy with the lowered standard of living?

AMY. Who decides who is pulling their own weight? You?

CHARLES. Yes, of course. Objective, non-biased people like myself.

(Everyone in the room looks at Charles in amazed disbelief).

PRISCILLA. Do you think that a Capitalist investor who lolls about on a beach drinking pina coladas is pulling his weight if she invested inherited cash and lives on the dividends from these investments?

CHARLES. This Capitalist performs a necessary function, so. Yes, I do.

FATHER. I don't believe that you possess any more of an objective, non-biased judgment about capitalism than anyone else in this room.

CHARLES. That's your opinion. You have always expressed doubts about the possibility of objectivity.

FATHER. Yes, specifically about yours.

PRISCILLA. How do you plan to get rid of the "unproductive" people?

CHARLES. I'd do nothing drastic. As I've previously indicated, I'd let the laws of nature squeeze them out of existence. If they didn't become productive, they wouldn't eat. They would disappear like the Dodo did.

FATHER. Dodos didn't disappear through starvation. Humans, who, I believe, used them for food deliberately killed them.

PRISCILLA. You are a murdering psychopath who deserves the agony of God's wrath. !

AL. I don't see why you're so upset. You want to see the earth cleared of people too.

PRISCILLA. (*A bit defensively*). I only want to send the righteous to a better place, and the evil ones, (she glares at Charles) to their well-deserved punishment. I've been helping the poor just as long as you say you have. The difference between us is that you have been giving them a free lunch, while I give them something more precious than money. I provide food, clothing, and shelter, and then encourage them to hear the Gospel. You demand nothing of them, except their vote. You provide them only with monetary aid. I provide them not only with food but also with an improved character and attitude. Our economic problems involve more than money, and I address these problems while you ignore them.

FATHER. I believe Priscilla has stumbled on an idea we may all find profitable. I'm not sure I understand exactly what you mean by character. In fact, I'm not sure you do either, but I agree that character, attitude, and values play a role in all human endeavors, including economic ones. Attitude, to me, is more important than facts. It is more important than our circumstances, giftedness, or skills. We cannot change the past. We cannot change the fact that people will act in a certain way. The only thing we can do is play the one string we have, and that's our attitude. *(Charles Swindoll) I, for one, would like to hear your ideas about how character and moral inclinations affect the economy, Priscilla.

PRISCILLA. While Charles was bragging about how superior his facts were, you Father, pointed out how many inaccurate facts were born out of honest mistakes or self-delusion. You ignored all the inaccuracies intentionally created by businesses and governments to deceive the public, the customer, and the investor... though the greedy investor deserves what he gets. The reason the economy fell apart isn't that various people perceived the facts differently, but because some people tried to cheat others by hiding the facts. If you really want to find the source of an economy's success or failure, you need to look no further than the level of corruption that lies behind it.

FATHER. (*Looks interested*).

PRISCILLA. A tiny country like Singapore developed a healthy economy and a high standard of living even though it possessed few natural resources because its economy is rooted in a system that rewards honesty and conscientiously follows the rule of law. People expect that the government will deal honestly and honorably with them, and the government, in turn, expects the people to deal with each other in the same manner. If they do not, they are punished severely. On the other hand, there are many basket-case economies in Africa that possess extensive natural resources, and the cheap labor capitalists seem to adore. According to Charles, these economies should be expanding at a good clip, and their standard of living should continually be improving faster than Singapore's because they have the 'real" building blocks of a healthy economy.

FATHER. (*Nods*). There is a lot of truth in what you are saying, Priscilla.

PRISCILLA. Instead, they are stuck in an economic quagmire where almost everyone participates as the victim or perpetrator of some form of corruption. Government officials take bribes from companies who want to ensure low prices for raw materials or to gain monopoly status within the country. On the streets, the police take bribes to do their jobs or to look the other way when a crime is committed. Farmer's and small business people must pay bribes or protection money in order to conduct business. This, of course, creates a stumbling economy. Almost everyone is bribing or extorting money from the weak and powerless. The people at the top, your "winners" or "survivors" as you call them, (she glances over at Charles), provide the model that everyone else tries to emulate. It would be foolish to do otherwise in such corrupt societies. If you want to solve our economic problems, Al, you should look at yourself and your cronies. You need to eliminate the corruption of business and government leaders before you can ever hope to heal the economy. You must stop the elite from taking advantage of the less fortunate and stop the less fortunate from preying on each other. Only then can our economy prosper.

CHARLES. The problem with Africa is not simply a matter of public corruption or human selfishness. Selfishness is often portrayed as being worse than it really is in Africa. Africa's biggest problem is its explosive population growth. In 1990 it was 634,000,000. Today it is already 984,000,000. This accelerating population growth has increased unemployment drastically. It has strained its health and educational infrastructure, and lowered the average person's standard of living. Disease has also spread as a result of the increased population. Africa simply does not possess enough financial resources to accommodate its residents. People must now struggle to find these. This constant competition for financial resources has as much to do with Africa's abundance of bribery as garden variety human selfishness does. Other countries have also experienced these problems but have been able to work their way out of them. For example, Indonesia and India have also seen exponential population growth, and their economies are humming right along. There is hope for Africa if African governments train their citizens to utilize the capital and the resources they have at hand more effectively. Africa exhibits a great deal of waste and hasn't invested wisely in human capital. Economic planning has been rudimentary at best, and governments haven't shown the kind of leadership that creates winners. Instead, it cultivates attitudes and priorities that produce losers.

FATHER. There is some truth in Charles' evaluation too.

PRISCILLA. No!

Africa's primary problem is corrupt leaders, and there is no hope for Africa as long as these incompetent criminals remain in power.

CHARLES. Incompetence and corruption go hand in hand. Inadequate planning wastes resources, and this creates scarcity. Scarcity intensifies competition for these resources, and this intense competition creates an environment where corruption can flourish. In such a situation, the fittest are not usually the most ethical or law-abiding. The only law everyone must follow in such an environment is the law of the jungle.

Al Which means no human law at all.

FATHER. You still haven't explained how Singapore was able to avoid such an environment, and I suspect that people follow many laws other than the law of the jungle in Africa. I think you've lost sight of your objective facts again, Charles.

PRISCILLA. Don't try to tell me why African economies are so weak. I know why from experience, real-life experience Father, not experience from one of Charles' textbooks. The primary causes of Africa's economic troubles are corrupt leaders, plain and simple. As you know, my church operates a mission in Africa. The mission consists of a small school and a health clinic that offers its services to the people of nearby villages for free. I've visited the mission twice and have seen with my own eyes how government corruption sucks the very life out of the economy. The government takes as much as it can from the people while giving back nothing. As a result, General Tsombe and his cronies drive around in new Mercedes while the people starve and die from easily preventable diseases.

CHARLES. I acknowledge that corruption is rampant in Africa, but that isn't the fault of. The economic system that operates within these countries is more like a brutal form of Feudalism. Few Capitalists want to make business investments there because they are afraid that government leaders will simply take anything that proves to be profitable.

PRISCILLA. And yet some Capitalists do invest there to source raw materials, and in so doing, keep Tsombe's military well funded so he can remain in power. Their profit-seeking and moral indifference support his monstrous greed and cruelty. As I said before, it's all about the lack of character.

AL. Governments in the rest of the world generally don't govern in the manner that this General Tsombe does, Priscilla. The situation you describe doesn't reflect the nature of government so much as it does the sinfulness of Tsombe.

PRISCILLA. Exactly! That's my point. The success or failure of all earthly economic systems boils down to individual people's character and their level of corruption. I did more through my mission to improve both the economic and spiritual health of Africans than either your capitalism, Charles, or your socialism Amy and certainly more than our government has done. My mission was the one bright light for the local people. Unfortunately, General Tsombe wants me to close it down.

AL. (*Suddenly looks concerned*). Have you been dabbling in politics again, Priscilla?

PRISCILLA. Tsombe murdered the former president, and his death squads continue to eliminate anyone who opposes him. Someone has to stand up to him when everyone else is afraid to do so.

AMY. Aren't you afraid?

PRISCILLA. Yes, but I know that God and moral right are on my side. God will punish this evil man. That is certain!

AL. (*His face reflecting both understanding and concern*). How has Tsombe responded to your opposition?

PRISCILLA. (Her voice rises). Two nights ago some of Tsombe's soldiers broke into the clinic and carried off two of the nurses....(*She finally breaks down and sobs*). Only God knows what those poor girls are going through now. When the pastor went to the local colonel in charge of these troops to learn the girls' fate, the colonel replied by laughing at him while telling him that he was taking all of the clinic's medical supplies because his troops needed them more than the pastor's parishioners did. He told him he had two days to hand over the supplies, shut down the mission, and leave the country.

FATHER. That was two days ago. Have the pastor and his staff arrived back in the United States yet?

PRISCILLA. I told the pastor and the remaining staff to hold their ground and give up nothing. We will not retreat in the face of evil!

(*The rest of the group looks at each other in stunned silence. Finally, Charles speaks, up*).

CHARLES. The only thing you accomplished was to sign the death warrant for your pastor and whoever stands with him.

AL. Yes, the soldiers will return, kill everyone, and take what they want. You gain nothing from this; the only result is unnecessary death.

AMY. My God Priscilla, how could you allow this to happen? You've killed them all!

AL. When you value souls more than you do people, you become another source of the world's suffering instead of one of its solutions. You may not see it, Priscilla, but you've made yourself Tsombe's partner in the pain that will occur when you combined your rigid attitude about your so-called principles with his violence and cruelty.

PRISCILLA. I'm not killing anyone. Tsombe is. I'm only offering the pastor a martyr's crown. His sacrifice will, I am sure, eventually, bring down Tsombe. I'm letting the pastor die for the sake of what is right and good. It is a glorious death.

AMY. If it is such an honor, why didn't you go back to Africa to take the pastor's place?

Priscilla"(*Her face turns bright red as she begins a slow burn. She leans forward from her seat as though she were about to grab Amy*).

AL. I wouldn't have gone back either. I don't fault you for that, but I would have told the pastor and remaining staff to abandon the mission and leave the country as quickly as possible, but then I don't have your "good" character, do I?

PRISCILLA. Of course, you wouldn't have. That's how you and I differ, you unbelieving, dissembling, vacillating, ungodly, selfish con artist!

AL. If I had been in charge, the pastor and the others could have lived to save souls another day. Sometimes the best response to a new problem is not to hold fast too to old beliefs. There is no dishonor in a strategic retreat.

FATHER. Yes, there is no lack of character in changing your beliefs when the old ones create more problems then they solve.

PRISCILLA. You know nothing about honor. None of you do.

AL. At least I hope you see that I'm not a General Tsombe. I have sincerely tried to limit some of our economy's corruption. I've already eliminated some of the abuses in lending and investing that led to the financial crisis. I've taken critical first steps in preventing people from taking advantage of each other. General Tsombe wouldn't have even considered doing that.

PRISCILLA. You are not the appropriate one to reform the economy because you believe in nothing more than your own survival and, as such, are too mired in this world's corruption. As Amy pointed out, you've proven yourself a poor role model for the rest of us. You have lost our faith and trust. Only Christ can serve as an appropriate role model.

AL. There's a difference between getting your hands dirty and being dirty. * (Line from "Luther" TV show).

FATHER. I can certainly understand your reluctance to believe in (*Al grimaces*), but he may be all you really have. Christ might make a good role model for integrity, but how likely will he return to make the specific economic decisions needed to extricate us from our current problems? While Charles overstates the importance of facts and financial laws, they must be considered in any financial solution. Your reliance on pure faith also seems misplaced and of limited utility, but should not be dismissed either. Amy, on the other hand, appears to be seeking economic solutions that combine both faith in other people and a necessary pragmatism. Do you think that she could better lead us out of this mess than Al?

PRISCILLA. Good grief, no! In her own way, she is just as much a sinner as Al. I can't place my faith in anyone who0 can be corrupted so easily. Both Al and Amy have been irrevocably corrupted.

FATHER. Why can't they atone for their errors and become useful leaders. I doubt that your Christ would agree that any human error is unforgivable. You have the capability and responsibility to value them differently when they change.

CHARLES. (*Smiles sardonically*). Of course, you could just "perceive" Al to be an incorruptible leader and follow him wherever he wants to go. He might even convince you that he has already moved the economy into your kingdom of god.

PRISCILLA. That's as unlikely as me modeling myself after Amy, or any of you modeling yourselves after Christ.

FATHER. Why do you always judge Amy so harshly? She obviously has a good heart.

PRISCILLA. (*Looks grimly at Amy, who looks terrified, as she shakes her head "NO"*). You think that the help she gives her friends is such a wonderful, selfless gesture, don't you?

FATHER. It sounds better than helping only those who agree with your particular religious beliefs.

PRISCILLA. Amy has been supporting a guy who left his wife and quit his job, so he doesn't have to pay child support.

AL. So, Amy has a new boyfriend. There's nothing earth shattering about that.

PRISCILLA. He hasn't worked in nine months. He just lies around Amy's flat, smoking marijuana and sinning with Amy.

AMY. There are no good-paying jobs that his training has prepared him to perform.

AL. The labor market IS tight.

PRISCILLA. I told you he quit his job. He doesn't want to work.

AMY. His previous employer didn't recognize his talents and stuck him in a low-level desk job.

FATHER. What type of work was he trained to do?

AMY. He's a CPA. His wife has been harassing him to take a job just like his last one. She set up a job interview with an old friend of hers. Of course, he's not going to go. She's no longer part of his life. She needs to accept this!

FATHER. (*Looks sadly at Amy*) He's not even going to see what the job is like? People have to try.

AMY. He's very special, very creative. He wants a job that utilizes all his skills.

CHARLES. I doubt that such a job exists.

FATHER. He's still married to his wife?

PRISCILLA. Yes, and she's trying to raise two small children.

FATHER. How do you know this?

PRISCILLA. She and the children are still members of my church. Amy met her husband there before she and the husband left the church to live in sin.

FATHER. Amy, this man has a wife and children to support. She's not out of his life at all.

AMY. She should be. He and I love each other. No one else loves us the way we do each other. None of you can understand how beautiful that is. Our love is a temple; (our) love is a higher law. * (Bono). Priscilla tries to make something beautiful look ugly.

FATHER. (*Sadly*). That's because you can only see your situation from the inside of it.

CHARLES. (*Chuckling*). It doesn't sound like your church has had much of a permanent influence on Amy and her new beau.

AL. Nothing ever comes between Amy and love.

PRISCILLA. My church has been providing food to the family through our food pantry. Without the groceries we provide the family they would go hungry. He refuses to help them in any way. People have stopped donating as much to the food pantry as they did before the financial crash - which Al did nothing to prevent. Soon we won't have any food left to give to this, or other needy families.

FATHER. What will happen to this family when the food runs out?

Pricilla: Their fate will be out of my hands. There will be nothing more that I can do. The food pantry was never designed to provide a permanent solution to persisting poverty, especially to a family abandoned by an able bodied breadwinner.

FATHER. At least you attempted to help these people in this life rather than wait for the next one. Perhaps you hold out more hope for this world's improvement than you let on.

PRISCILLA. This world can't be saved. The good deeds I do on earth will be feeble and temporary, while the glory of the next world will be permanent and substantial.

AL. I, too, admire what you've done to help these families. (*Priscilla manages a smile*). Temporary relief is better than no relief at all, even if ultimately you lack faith in the ability of rest of us to develop more substantial economic solutions in the here and now.

FATHER. Amy, you, on the other hand, say you want to help others, and yet you've done nothing but hurt this man's family. Didn't you say earlier that we could escape this economic crisis if we helped each other? Name one thing you've done to help this man's wife and children. (*He raises his eyes to look Amy in the face*).

AMY. (*A bit flustered*). Ah..... after Bob moved in with me, she..... became really angry and nasty to us. She's never liked me from the start. She likes me less now. She left a message on my answering machine, calling me a home-wrecking slut. (*Priscilla nods with approval, and Father sighs*). How can you expect me to help someone that ugly and hurtful? She doesn't want my help. She just wants to make our lives miserable. I avoid her as much as I can. I can't avoid and help her at the same time. It's physically impossible.

CHARLES. (*Nods*). Yes, that's logical.

FATHER. You admit that she and her children need help?

AMY. Yes, but I can't help her. She cares nothing about my feelings.

FATHER. She has feelings too. Did you care about hurting her feelings when you became involved with her husband?

AMY. Ah... (*She starts to cry*) It's all too painful.

FATHER. Yes it is, and you're partly responsible for this pain

CHARLES. Amy, I knew you'd eventually come around to my point of view. See how easy it is to become heartless?

AMY. Heartless? I love him. No one can feel more love than I do.

CHARLES. You don't love his wife and children, though, do you? How much do you "feel" for them? I'd guess not much more than I did for the people I had to lay off to keep my business afloat.

AMY. I ...hurt someone because I loved someone else. You love nothing.

AL. Except, possibly business success.

FATHER. You could help her. You could buy food with your unemployment check to give to Priscilla's food pantry, and Priscilla could pass it on to her. You can help her secretly if you don't want to deal with her directly.

AMY. I still don't like her. She's not a nice person.

PRISCILLA. What are you?

AMY. I want to help my friends, and she certainly is not a friend. Your government programs, Al, are supposed to help her instead of me. Why do I need to be the one to help?

FATHER. You're the one who contributed to her problem.

AMY. She should apply for welfare or food stamps. The government should do its job instead of passing it on to me.

PRISCILLA. You're the one who is passing on responsibility. You and people like you are one reason this economy isn't working properly. It's all about personal corruption,

AL. I can appreciate your wanting to pass on a task to government that you don't feel you can handle, but you've completely demolished your idea that the economy can be saved if people will only help and support each other. If you won't follow your own advice, who will? How do you expect people who don't even begin to believe in your outlook, (*He looks over at Charles*), will follow it?

FATHER. Still, some elements of mutual support, and, I might add, ethical behavior probably needs to be added to whatever economic solutions you develop.

AMY. I'm sorry I've let everyone down. I don't want to hurt anyone. (*She continues to sob uncontrollably*).

PRISCILLA. And yet you do.

CHARLES. Don't worry about it, Amy. Hurting others is unavoidable. We're all competing for limited resources. Your boyfriend just happens at the moment to be one of those limited resources.

PRISCILLA. A very limited resource.

AL. (*Smiles, and tries to make a joke*). I'm not sure that boyfriends are much of a limited resource for Amy since she always seems to have one.

CHARLES. She is just one of the fittest competitors

Pricilla: In other words, an irresponsible sinner. (*Al and even Charles are embarrassed by Priscilla's cruelty, and neither respond to Priscilla's comment. Amy continues to sob*).

AL. This sad situation proves a point I've wanted to make.

AMY. (*Sniffs*). What is that?

AL. Corruption doesn't always start at the top and work its way down. Sometimes it moves in the opposite direction. The corruption of government may not be my fault. It might be everyone's.

FATHER. Possibly, but rather than drawing attention away from yourself, you need to focus on what part you may play in cultivating our corruption and eventual misery. That's the part you can really change.

AL. As should Priscilla, Charles, and Amy.

FATHER. Yes, everyone needs to learn how to better reject the indifference and heartlessness that encourages us to take advantage of each other.

AL. That won't happen unless someone can convince **them** that it is in their best interests to do so. Someone has to show them that greater access to wealth and a better standard of living is possible only if they clearly understand the big picture and resist twisting it into any shape they desire. That someone is me! (*He rises from his chair and stands ramrod straight in some sort of cheesy heroic pose.*)

PRISCILLA. The only way to make people do what their fallen nature resists is to force them to confront their eternal damnation. You must show them how God will punish them if they do not treat others appropriately. (*She looks at Amy and points a finger accusingly. Amy shrinks back*).

AMY. Daddy, What is the truth? Did I add to the world's problems, or am I just a victim of economic laws and forces that are beyond my control? Am I the villain or the victim?

AL. That's the question we should all be asking ourselves, isn't it.

FATHER. Yes, and the answer constantly changes. A surplus of people, a scarcity of resources, an unhealthy concentration of power, a heartless competition for wealth and attention, individual indifference, mass alienation, self-deception and a certainty that we are not responsible for any of it have all brought us the economic and personal misery that we are experiencing. These factors corrode our trust in others and corrupt our faith in the economy and in everyone who play a role in it. People can, of course, resist this corrosion. We have the ability to maintain faith in others while acknowledging our own shortcomings and lack of omniscience.

CHARLES. Such faith is impossible. My trust in reason has substance and a proven track record.

AMY. I don't care what's possible and what's not. My faith in people and in love has kept me on my feet (*Priscilla raises an eyebrow.*) and trying my best to continue on when Charles' reason and Priscilla's God have told me to stop. Neither reason nor God can make me become less or more than human.

AL. (*Sits thinking about Amy's last statement. His eyes light up.*)

SAINT AL?

AL. Maybe the economy can't be mended entirely, but it can be fixed well enough for all of us to get by. We just need faith that a solution exists even though it can't always be described clearly. (*He smiles at Priscilla, and she smiles back.*) We all need faith that I can put something together, and I can!

CHARLES. I can't believe in anything you propose if you plan to turn you back on economic facts and base everything you do on faith and fuzzy perceptions. All economic solutions are in plain sight; you just don't want to see or implement them. The solutions exist in the facts you refuse to face, not in faith.

AL. What if there are no unimpeachable economic facts from which I can build economic solutions? What if all economies are temporary, and none that have ever existed were perfect or should necessarily be used as economic models? What if your faith in facts is just as important and just as baseless as Priscilla's faith in her God? What if all your economic laws give you a false sense of certainty?

FATHER. (*Looks up at Al with surprise and admiration.*)

CHARLES. If we question the economic laws, we have worked so hard to discover all that will remain of our economy will be chaos and confusion.

No solutions are possible when we don't allow eternal economic truths to exist.

PRISCILLA. (*Deep in thought then nods her head*).

AL. Is it really the end of the world if we acknowledge all the exceptions to the rules that we actually experience during our economic transactions amongst ourselves? Wouldn't blind faith in your eternal laws divert our attention away from temporary solutions that might help us get by for a year or two and give us time to come up with some new though also temporary solution? If we are all living in an economic universe where final, permanent success is impossible according to the facts, shouldn't we still be able to cobble together some temporary solutions that ignore their long-term failure? Is it really impossible to reestablish trust and faith in an economy in the face of its inevitable decline?

AMY. How can we do that? How can we be optimistic enough to motor on and pessimistic enough to see the sheer drop off that lies ahead? I can't do that.

AL. You already know how to do it, Amy. We just need to treat the economy the same way you've dealt with the love affairs that deep down you knew would end in tears. You made believe you believed and did your best to make them work. You tried with all your heart. You honestly tried. You always had hope, no matter what past experience was whispering in your ear.

CHARLES. (*Snorts*). And when the economy goes over that cliff, what do you do then? This method always leads to failure. Why do you want to face failure over and over again?

AL. You face it because it is always there waiting to spring out and surprise you if you are not prepared for it. It is eternal, part of existence itself. It is hiding in your facts. It flits about your reason. You can't avoid it, so you must learn to deal with it. After your program fails, you try something a little different next time, and you accept whatever temporary success you did achieve. You accept that your success was never destined to last forever. You plan your next move, while never forgetting to live in the present and reap whatever you can from what you had previously sown.

PRISCILLA. We reap what we have sown, all right. You only sow lies, deceit, and falsehood, and I can believe in nothing that doesn't last forever. Only God lasts forever. Your plans, as usual, will crumble into dust and disappear. They can end only as an abject failure.

AMY. It's better to have loved and lost than never to have loved at all.

FATHER. Just as it's better to have lived and lost than never to have lived at all.

AL. I am not exactly sowing lies when I honestly try to make them true. After all, what is a lie? It's just the inverse of a fact and just as mutable. * Made-up solutions are not falsehoods if you admit that they might not work, and if they do work, they cannot continue to do so forever.

CHARLES. You will have sown false expectations, never the less, and your constituents will be disappointed with any failure that results. People will lose even more trust in you than they already have. They won't accept any future plans you might have. You and your economy will be dead in the water. There will be no resurrection of the economy and no reelection for you.

AL. If I do my job correctly, I will lead them from effort to effort, always demonstrating the possible utility of the next solution and the value and success of whatever we are currently attempting.

PRISCILLA. I know how you operate. When things go wrong, you will try to find someone or something other than yourself is to blame.

AL. (*Shrugs*) I might do that, but I will also draw a clear picture of why we need to follow some new solutions. I know from experience that this is an excellent way to proceed.

AMY. You would cast blame on some innocent person for your own mistake?

AL. I might have to if I wanted a second chance at making everything right, and how can you, of all people, Amy, condemn me for shrugging off blame?

AMY. (*Blushes and looks away from everyone*).

PRISCILLA. You have no shame. You will never become one of God's elect.

AL. God's not registered to vote. That's the election I care about.

AMY. When your plans fail, people will end up suffering. That's not fair. Can't you protect us from this suffering?

AL. I'll do my best, but no, I can't guarantee it. I'll admit that only to the people in this room. Perhaps people should look to Priscilla's God for that kind of hope, and I'm not that God. Still, people will probably benefit economically much more under my guidance than under her God's or under Charles' god of natural selection.

Neither regime would offer much hope for economic success or happiness in this life. Charles's heartless economic laws would lead us into a ruthless, brutal chaos instead of the rational stability he claims these laws provide.

If I follow his advice, we might, at best, end up with an economy resembling feudalism, and at worst, the predatory economy of animals in the natural world. Existence has the potential to be meaningful and pleasant if we exercise the imagination, thought, and faith that exists within each of us, and makes us human. I want to release that potential and the hope it provides as much as possible.

FATHER. (*Catches Al's eye and nods his head.*)

CHARLES. (*Laughs*).

PRISCILLA. Existence is a trial, a test to determine who is worthy of God's grace and mercy. Existence must be borne with dignity and contrition. Our reward for our piety will arrive in the next life, in God's kingdom. Anything you do to make people's lives more comfortable in this corrupt and fallen world just diverts their attention from the real prize that lies in the future.

FATHER. Not all Christians believe as you do. Christ showed mercy to those living in this world. He wanted people to live better lives in this world, not the next. Al seems to want to do the same thing.

PRISCILLA. Putting Al and Christ in the same sentence is sacrilege.

FATHER. Perhaps Christ was a lot less concerned about his own well-being Than Al is. I'll grant you that, but ...

PRISCILLA. (*Interrupts*). When he was nailed on the cross between the two thieves who would not repent, he realized that he had failed. It is his resurrection and promises to save those who believe in this miraculous resurrection that forms the foundation of my Christianity, not the reform and improvement of this world. The hope that Christianity provides revolves around not this world but the paradise that awaits all who believe.

FATHER. Your beliefs are as ridiculous as Marx's promise of the inevitability of the Dictatorship of the Proletariat in some distant future.

AL. Yes, placing your solutions in a place that no one has actually experienced or can otherwise test, accomplishes nothing and only justifies the cruelty, smugness, and heartlessness exhibited in this life by some of the so-called guardians of your faith.

PRISCILLA. A confirmed liar like you dares to apply those terms to me. They are all lies, and you are nothing but a selfish, lying, and self-centered politician.

AL. (*Shrugs*). I'm a lot of things, but I'm willing to change. Are you?

AMY. Al says he cares about me, and I believe him because he has a reason to care. He knows I wouldn't vote for him otherwise. You care nothing about me personally, only about my soul. Al, you and I have probably messed up from time to time, and we may have created more problems than we've solved, but I trust that you really want to try to make things right just as I do. I believe you intend to fix the economy.

Neither Charles' immutable law of the jungle nor Priscilla's God will be much help to me and the people I know. You're all we can rely on. I believe in you even if these two don't, because….because I have to believe that someone cares about me.

FATHER. I fear that after talking all afternoon, we're still unable to reach any common ground.

Al sits thinking while lightly touching the five fingers of one hand with the same fingers on the other. He looks at the space he has created between them. Then he clears his throat.

AL. I think you are wrong, Pops. Charles, it would be a shame if the Economic Development council cancels that business loan you currently have.

CHARLES. You would have them cancel my loan? You are one nasty snake!

AL. No, no, not me. I've heard some rumors that several Council members don't like you much. In fact, I don't recall lately running into anyone, anywhere who indicated they like you.

CHARLES. I'm a rational businessman, not an applicant in some popularity contest.

AL. They not only don't like you, but they don't trust you either. The Council distributes those loans to firms that will improve the health of the economy as a whole. For some reason, they think that your business is a cutthroat operation that will not help other ones start-up or expand. They are under the impression that you care only about the survival of your own particular business, and nothing else.

AMY. They do so with good reason, don't they? See, I know how to be reasonable too.

AL. I could help you out. We've had our disagreements in the past, but you are my brother, after all. I have a family obligation to help you. Several members of the Council owe me a favor. I could put in a good word for you...If you'd like.

PRISCILLA. Another dirty de You really don't know how to get and stay clean, do you?

AL. (*Ignores her*). Of course, if you don't trust me, you can always operate your business without the loan. I'm sure you could sell some of that gold you've got stored away to finance your new business. Oh, wait! That would mean you would have to assume all the risks for the company yourself. I'm sure you have no problem with that. Risks are what capitalists take. Right? And as one of the fittest, you should be able to survive with no government help at all. (He cackles mischievously.)

CHARLES. (*Swallows nervously*).

AL. Unfortunately, we have no way of knowing if that's true until a few years down the road. Or, maybe we can gather some ideas right now. You'll have to cash in your gold investment at a substantial loss, won't you? That would make you an immediate loser, one of the unfit, no longer a good candidate for survival I'll bet that you don't want to admit that you don't deserve a spot on your island of light and rationality.

CHARLES. All right, you've made your point. I'll accept your help. Knowing you, you'll want something in return. What is it? Stock options? A campaign contribution? An outright cash bribe?

AL. (*Smiles*). I want you to hire Amy.

CHARLES. (*Stunned*). To do what?

AL. To serve as the public face of your company. Your face is doing it no favors.

FATHER. (*Smiles as though he has caught on to Al's plan.*).

PRISCILLA. I don't see it as much of an improvement.

AL. Amy will represent your company at all future meetings with the Economic Development Council. She will lead all of your company's public relations efforts.

CHARLES. We don't have any.

AL. You do now.

AMY. I don't want to work for Charles. He really doesn't care about anything except the success and survival of his business; I'll have to lie when I pretend he feels otherwise.

AL. Is that really so difficult for you? Really? Think how much fun it will be to organize plant tours for school children so they can see how Charles makes….whatever it is he makes. You can single-handedly inspire them to study hard so that someday they might start and operate a business just like Charles', or, more likely, that someday they might work in such a place. You'd be teaching again, and helping others. You'll be meeting lots of people and developing cooperative agreements among them. Isn't that what you really want?

AMY. Well, yes, I think so.

AL. You won't be lying when you translate whatever Charles' research firm does into language that everyone can understand. You'll be making it clearer. (*Grins*). Perhaps you would be making it clearer for Charles too. But Amy, you'll have to do something for me before I make Charles hire you.

AMY. I think I'll like this new teaching job. OK, what do I have to do?

AL. Promise to give Priscilla part of your salary so she can continue to operate her food bank.

PRISCILLA. What makes you think I would take Amy's money?

CHARLES. Do you really want your parishioners to go hungry while you wait for your hoped-for end of days?

FATHER. Would Christ have done that?

AL. You can't turn your back on the world when your feet are still planted firmly upon it.

PRISCILLA. I.....all right, I'll take the donations, but she must donate at least 15% of her salary. That would be an appropriate tithe.

CHARLES. Heh, she turns to face the world and immediately begins to negotiate with it. You're learning fast, Priscilla.

AMY. Why should I give 15% of my salary when the members of your flock only give 10%?

PRISCILLA. I added the extra so you could better redeem yourself in the eyes of God. (*Amy rolls her eyes*).

AL. Do you really want to deny your boyfriend's children some powdered milk and eggs? They don't deserve to go hungry, do they?

AMY. No.

AL. Didn't you have one of his children in your class before you were laid off?

AMY. (*Quietly*) Yes, Michelle.

AL. Was she a bad student? Did she disrupt the class and make you angry?

AMY. (*Very quietly*). No, she was a good student, very sweet and nice.…..
All right, stop it. I'll give whatever part of my salary Priscilla wants. I only
have one condition. I don't want Bryon's wife, or anyone else to know that
I'm doing this. People will think I feel guilty about living with Bryon,
and….I don't!

PRISCILLA. Don't worry about that. I don't want anyone to know that
I still have anything to do with you.

AL. Yes, Priscilla, a little deceit can sometimes be a very beneficial and
lovely thing. (*Looks around the room*). Priscilla, find out if your pastor and
his staff are still alive in Africa, and fly them someplace where they are
safe. I'll give you the money for their plane fare.

PRISCILLA. (*She snorts.*) Take money from you?

FATHER. If you won't take it from him, I'll give it to you. If you acknowledge that martyrdom is often a waste of human life that repairs nothing.

PRISCILLA. (*Thinks for a moment*). No, I'll take it from him.

AL. We are all in agreement?

CHARLES. (*Glaring at Al*). Yes.

PRISCILLA. (*Still considering Father's last comment*). I agree.

AMY. (*Smiling broadly*). Yep! I like this arrangement a lot. We're finally
all helping each other just as I proposed, aren't we? (Amy goes over to
Charles and shakes his hand). Boss, when do you want me to start work?

CHARLES. (*Sighs*) Tomorrow morning at 8 a.m.

AMY. (*Walks over to Priscilla and looks down at her feet*) I never meant to hurt anyone Thank you for allowing me to make up for it. (*She goes to her father and hugs him*). Daddy, you are always so wise. (*Finally, she goes over to Al and hugs him too*) My hero! You've performed the impossible! I'll never forget your help and support. (She waves to the group as she bounces to the door). I can't wait to tell Bryon about the new job. Now we can have some nice things. (*She leaves the room*).

PRISCILLA. (*Smiling for the first time of the day*). You think you're pretty clever, don't you, Al? (*Al smiles and shrugs*). But you haven't fixed everyone's problems, have you?

FATHER. It's never possible to repair everything.

AL. It may, in fact, be impossible to repair anything back to its original condition. What of it?

PRISCILLA. You let Amy walk out of here while still living in sin with another woman's husband. Why couldn't you fix that?

AL. If it's a problem, it might be one that will fix itself, don't you agree Pops?

FATHER. It's possible.

PRISCILLA. I don't see how...

CHARLES. Your religion certainly wasn't going to fix it.

AL. Amy isn't going to listen to anything anyone might have to say about her relationship, so why try...but Charles, don't you have a number of young men working as research assistants for your firm?

CHARLES. (*Oblivious to where this is going*). Yes, so?

PRISCILLA. (*Who immediately catches on*). Young single men?

CHARLES. Yes.

AL. Then, I'm sure you will allow nature to take its course. That is your philosophy, correct? Those industrious young men will start looking better and better to Amy over time, and her stay-at-home-lay-about worse and worse. Amy's salary will undoubtedly improve her lot, but knowing you, I doubt you are going to be paying Amy so much that she can afford any luxuries.

CHARLES. Certainly not!

AL. And her contribution to Priscilla's food bank should keep her on a tight budget. I think that eventually, she will tire of baking a cake every time she wants her hair done. We all know Amy. She will move on.

PRISCILLA. Thank God!

CHARLES. No, thank the invisible hand of supply and demand. (*He rises*). I expect you to keep your part of the bargain. I'll fire Amy the moment you betray me.

AL. Don't worry.

CHARLES. (*Nods and leaves*).

Priscilla; (*Slaps her knees as she gets up*). You two have created a little bit of prosperity for all of us. A bit of a miracle, isn't it?

FATHER. I haven't done much except listen. This was all Al's doing.

PRISCILLA. For some reason, I feel your presence has done more than that. (*She leaves*).

FATHER. (*Turns to Al*). How long do you think your arrangement will last? A month? A year? Longer?

AL. It only has to last long enough to give me some time to think up the next arrangement. We both know that no solution will last forever. We can't ever know if any answer is the best one, but we have to do something, don't we? That's the philosophy you're always preaching.

FATHER. (*nods in agreement*). That part's true, but you will need a long-term strategy that you honestly believe before you can fix the broader economy. You must believe in something other than yourself, even if these beliefs change over time. A few self-doubts could save you from making some terrible mistakes. Do you really want to fall into mental traps that your sisters and brother often fall into? I fear that you leave here today in worse shape than when you came.

AL. Cobbling something together as I go along *is* my long-term strategy, and I **now** know I can succeed with this strategy. I now know that I am capable of anything!

FATHER. (*Shudders*) You've learned nothing from today's discussion. I liked you better when you were uncertain about what to do next. I certainly trusted you more. (*Sighs*). At least I hope you've come to see that as a politician, you have a choice. You can simply represent your constituency and take them somewhere they already want to go, which might harm them, or you can lead them to someplace they never considered where they might end up benefiting a lot more. You understand you have that choice, right? You can lead or follow. It's up to you.

AL. I only know that to be re-elected, I have to appear to be trying to make things work, and if people believe I'm trying, then whatever I come up with **will** work.

Perceptions are more important than facts, right Pops? You helped me find the confidence I need to stay in the game. By closeting me here with those three, you gave me a chance to see the weakness of their inflexible points of view, and the dead ends that result from them. I noticed that there are no permanent solutions that can be reliably manufactured from some firmly believed orthodoxy. Confidence and action, almost any action, forms the only path to success. You've given me the confidence to never give up trying to make people believe in me.

FATHER. You say you understand the importance of never giving up, and trying to appear to be a leader. Are you really trying to be a leader if you don't honestly believe that your efforts will actually produce more long-term benefits for your constituents, than for you? Appearances are not enough. The economy needs a good gardener, and a good gardener requires a spirit of dedication. Do you possess that spirit?

AL. (*Al in his excitement, barely hears him*). If I can get those three to work together, I'm certain I can persuade my colleagues to agree on bigger and better economic solutions, whatever they might be, and convince my constituents that they have nothing to fear. I have my mojo back. I can already taste a victory in November. I'm ready to move forward again. (*He jumps up from his chair.*) Pops, I don't need you anymore. Thanks (*He leaves the room with a bouncing step. He stubs his toe at the door, and then carries on.*).

FATHER. (*Sits alone amid his library*). What have I done? What proud beast stumbles toward Bethlehem waiting to be born? * (Paraphrase W.B.Yeats)

www.ingramcontent.com/pod-product-compliance
Lightning Source LLC
Chambersburg PA
CBHW070331220526
45467CB00001B/112